Musings and Philosophy
of an Iowa Farmer

Musings and Philosophy of an Iowa Farmer

Jere Probert

iUniverse, Inc.
New York Bloomington Shanghai

Musings and Philosophy of an Iowa Farmer

Copyright © 2008 by Jere Probert

iUniverse books may be ordered through booksellers or by contacting:

iUniverse
1663 Liberty Drive
Bloomington, IN 47403
www.iuniverse.com
1-800-Authors (1-800-288-4677)

ISBN: 978-0-595-52395-5 (pbk)
ISBN: 978-0-595-62447-8 (ebk)

Printed in the United States of America

Contents

Acknowledgements

It seems some books have glowing acknowledgements. They are so glowing that it is as if they have gone beyond being credible. If mine are anything, they are credible.

Had it not been for two dedicated people this book would not have happened. Nearly everything in this book was written to please myself or meet some inner need that could not be met any other way. There are several items in it that are about sad circumstances, or at least I perceived them to be sad circumstances. I achieved great relief by writing them. They were written selfishly. Most of them were carelessly scrawled on a yellow legal pad. Some were written on scraps of paper that happened to be there at the right time. Through the years my wife and my brother encouraged each effort.

Beverly Probert, my wife, kept every single scrap of paper I had written on. My brother, William F. Probert, is a continual encouragement. The two of them convinced me that each item had value. Sometimes they even suggested a topic. The title of one of the stories is "By Request." "Wintering 100 Head of Cattle" is the result of another request.

One winter when the pile of scraps had gotten much bigger, and I had gotten much older, Beverly typed them all and put them on a flash drive. In the meantime, William found a woman who would edit the stories and guide us through the process. He brought the third person into the acknowledgement group. She is known to me as Carol Lacy. Carol is the one who edited for us and guided us through the process.

My thanks to the three of you.

Introduction

1

The School Board Member

Jere Probert, School Board Member
Valley Community School District & Keystone Area Education Agency

I thought it might be in the best interest of society for me to identify myself, so that if you meet me you will recognize me. There are thousands of me in Iowa alone, freely roaming about. Physically, I am small and tall, overweight and underweight; I'm the picture of health and terminally ill; I am male and female; my skin is every beautiful color that God chose to allow one of His creations to have. I'm a health nut, and I take terrible care of myself; I'm probably a parent, but I may be childless.

Politically, I'm either a Republican or Democrat, except when I am a third-party member, unaffiliated or disinterested. I'm extremely liberal, extremely conservative, middle-of-the-road, and tired of labels.

I'm the storied doctor, lawyer, and Indian chief as well as housewife, retiree, farmer, banker, laborer, and am self-employed. I will work at anything. Despite what you may have heard, my spouse is not a school administrator; my spouse, though, may work at any profession also. I am naive, idealistic and opinionated.

I am a board member because the voters in my community asked me personally to oversee the educational system in which their children are participating. They did this because of my personal integrity, my business sense, my interest in education, or for some other real or imagined trait they think they see in me. They know that I will put in the necessary time, without charge, and in some cases, my spouse may even give up a position within the school, so that I can serve.

Somewhere, in the middle of my first term, I began to pick up character traits that were new to me; I learned to listen—to listen to parents (calm, partly angry, and out of control), principals, teachers, children of all ages, bus drivers, and bridge crews. I discovered the art of compromise. I learned the need for procedures. I learned to accept praise and insults from people at the local, area-wide, and state levels with my tongue in my cheek.

In this age of special interest groups, I think that I am a member of the most important one. You see, I have a special interest in the people of this nation who are in the process of earning their formal education. There is no way that you could make me have that interest by paying me. One of the few ways in which you could insult me is to imply that I have some illegal or corrupt self-serving reason for doing this. The reasons I do it are self-serving, but in a different way. Because of this job, I am a different person, more aware of my fellow beings' needs and capabilities, and therefore, am more able to be what I was intended to be. That makes it the ultimate self-indulgence: fun.

2

Pen Is in Hand, a Dry Run

The process begun!
Head full of words
Get ready for fun!
Grab your hat
Hang on to your clothes
Three to get ready
So here it goes!

3

The Stories I Tell: A Disclaimer

The stories I tell are from a time when
Women were women and ladies were ladies.
Farmers didn't go broke
Like they did in the eighties.
Before peace protestors, flower children,
And environmental enlightenment
When no one had a problem.
With the placement of bovine excrement.
We thought it to be a
Natural proceeding,

Considering the amount
Those critters were eating.
The stories I tell are true stories
As best I remember
Since I bumped my head last October,
Or was it September?

4

One Can Be Inspired

One can be inspired.
One can be retired.
Neither will happen
Unless one perspired.

5

On Getting Published

I've written some things of which I'm proud,
Getting something published was my goal.
Nothing I tried seemed to work.
Do publishers have a soul?
There was this poet I heard,
I'd go again if he ever came back.
Surely he would recognize my talent.
His name is Baxter Black.
I mailed him my best.
Now I'm on the right track.
At least he saved on postage.
He didn't mail it back.
He wrote me a nice note
To help to ease the pain.
The note was three lines long.
He said they needed rain.
In May of 89, we mailed one to *Reader's Digest*.
They used it; I'll never be the same.
They published it all right …
In my daughter's married name.

6

Strangely Silent

At a time when you'd least expect it,
At a time of emotion,
At a time of turmoil,
At a time you'd least expect it, this pen is strangely quiet.
At a time I thought I was threatened, and couldn't deny it,
At a time of concern,
At a time of fright,
At a time when I really needed it, this pen was strangely quiet.
At a time of sorrow, when I cried about it,
At a time of grief,
At a time of wonder,
At a time when I cried about it, this pen was strangely quiet.
At a time of land sales, when I didn't want to do it,
At a time of failure,
At a time of defeat,
At a time when I was afraid to try it, this pen was strangely quiet.
Were those times I was emotionally greedy?
Were those times of self pity?
Were those times I should follow Him?
Were those times when if I'd try it, He'd write it?
And the Pen is not strangely silent!!!

7

Please Don't Ask Me That

Sometimes they smell of Genius,
But there are others
That are best read rapidly
While holding your nose.
Some are inspired
Some should never have prospered
Which gave rise to the phrase
Anonymously authored.

Section I
The Farm

1

Here in Section Nineteen

Crossing my mind, the other day in sort of a foggy mist,
Was a thought; not that that is particularly remiss.
What am I doing here? Thinking, of course, from the point of geography.
Much shallower than theology or some Greek philosophy.
What am I doing here?
In section nineteen.

How come I am right here?
Where three generations of Scots lived and prospered and grew old and died.
Some of them left, they found other things to do, and tried.
Is my reasoning somehow convoluted?
What they found here was easily accessible water.
Why am I here now? You can't drink it, it is all polluted.
In section nineteen.

They loved the woodlands, hardwood forests,
Raw material to build with, "The future is before us."
The forests have been cut and pastured.
They are gone long before they have matured.
In section nineteen

The bald eagle soars again
Carried on currents of the same old south wind.
They soar majestically above the bluffs,
Long ago named "Blauwearie" by the Probert's and the Duff's.
In section nineteen

The land in which they found hope, hope almost magical,
Has long since been declared by agriculturists, mostly marginal.
Mink Creek still winds close to where it has always been,
Where the hills meet the flats, it meanders the same now as then.
In section nineteen

In 1857, when the ancestors came,
There was great excitement, a new land to tame.
One hundred years later, with a world in need,

There was great excitement, a world to feed.
We would help.
In section nineteen

As the century and the millennium draw to a close
The population of the world grows and grows.
At government expense, we seed down exotic grasses,
And wonder what will be here when another century passes.
In section nineteen

With all of this thought and burdensome reflection,
Are we owning land to carry on a tradition?
The original question remains, I fear,
"What am I doing here?"
In section nineteen
Highland township
Clayton County, Iowa

Jack and Jean

2

Corn Picker's Memories and Stories

Our parents moved to a rather large, for the time, farm in Section 19, Highland Township, Clayton County, Iowa, in the early 1930s. The farm was a contiguous 960 acres comprised mostly of steep clay hills, woods, and a hundred acres of prime black bottomland. A normal crop year would see them planting more than a hundred acres of corn, eighty acres of oats, with the balance in hay and pasture. They rented on a standard fifty-fifty crop livestock lease. In some parts of the US this was known as "sharecropping." It was general farming with milk cows, beef cows, hogs, chickens, and purchased beef steers.

In the early days of this operation, labor-intensive operations—such as corn picking or manure handling—were done by hired labor. One year, two young men were hired to pick corn. One of them had a team of horses. He received $1.25 per day plus room and board for him and his team. The other man received $1.00 per day plus room and board. They were expected to take care of the horses, hand-pick and shovel into a crib, thirty bushels of corn in the morning and in the afternoon.

The late fall of 1939 saw Dad buy a new 1940 Model A John Deere Tractor with a John Deere 101 semi-mounted picker. Part of the weight of the unit was carried on the rear wheels of the tractor and the rest of it was carried on one wheel on the picker. He purchased a new Kewanee grain elevator to facilitate handling the grain. Times were changing and, in hindsight, it looks as if he was anticipating World War II. He also purchased a new 1940 Ford automobile.

As a young boy, sometime between 1940 and 1946, I witnessed the following: *One particularly rainy fall, Dad had difficulty negotiating the steep wet clay hills with the "A" and the 101. Front wheels would ball up with mud and corn residue until they refused to rotate. Rear wheels would spin out, pivoting the rear of the unit downhill off the rows. Wagon wheels did not want to cooperate either. Getting the corn into the picker was nearly impossible and if some ears got into the picker the chances of them ending up in the wagon were slim to none. We still had work horses at this time. Dad's horses were big, the one-ton variety of no known pedigree. They were well broke, experienced, and docile to a fault. His solution to the picking problem was to hitch the team to the front of the A. He then was in the position of running the team, the tractor, and the picker all at the same time. The horses were hooked directly to the front spindle, keeping the front wheels where they were supposed to be and furnishing enough extra pull to make the whole unit behave more appropriately.*

I have no knowledge of how many acres he picked that way, but I do know that is how he finished picking that year.

Many years, perhaps thirty years later, I remembered this story and asked Dad about it. He confirmed my memories. I asked him how he was able to control the team, the tractor, and the wagon all at the same time. He responded, "That was no problem, the team quickly learned what they were supposed to do; when I yelled 'Get Up' they started to pull and when they heard the snap of the hand clutch releasing they stopped."

By 1950, our tractor fleet had grown to include a 1947 GM and an H, as well as the 40 "A." During the summer of 1950, Dad traded those three tractors for a new A, B, and MC. The MC was a very small track-laying tractor. It had tracks instead of wheels. The A and B did not show up until 1951. Prior to this trade, the 101 had been traded for a Woods Brothers one-row pull-type picker. The hills were then more easily negotiated by the MC pulling the Woods picker. I have only one memory concerning this arrangement:

Again the story takes place on the steep clay-side hills. This time they were frozen and icy. Anyone familiar with the characteristics of a crawler tractor knows that they will go sideways on an icy hill as if they were on ice skates turned 90 degrees. This day, Dad came in with the seat completely removed from the crawler. He told me he had unhooked the wagon, pulled forward with the picker and disconnected it from the MC. He then drove the crawler above the wagon in preparation to bringing it home. Just as he was passing the wagon on the uphill side the MC took off sliding toward the wagon on the ice. He was nearly past the wagon and the seat struck the parked wagon removing the seat. Of course I asked, "What did you do?" His response? "I stood up."

The Woods was usually left in the field during the picking season. On occasion, inclement weather would cause the final elevator to freeze at the bottom. The solution for that was to drain some gasoline from the carburetor, gather some cornstalks and husks, drench them with the gasoline, and set them on fire under the elevator. Obviously this was done in a field of dry corn and cornstalks with the tractor hooked on the other end of the picker. By 1958, every component of the Woods picker had been welded or repaired in some manner at least once. Yields had passed its design capability, and it was time for a new John Deere 227 picker to slip on the 51 A.

Hearing that I had purchased a new Deere picker, an elderly neighbor and lifelong John Deere fan, told me the following story.

When John Deere first started making corn pickers a local salesman decided that he would hook a tractor to one and just drive from farm to farm to show it. It was not yet harvest season but he wanted to have some sold in advance of the season.

During his stop at one farm, he got a little carried away with his sales pitch. He said this picker will pick down corn. In fact, it will pick up ears of corn that are no longer attached to the stalk. At this statement, the farmer stopped him and told him that he did not believe any of this. Not to be deterred by anything, the salesman suggested that they go to the farmer's corn crib, get a bushel basket of corn, and just scatter it in the barnyard. He would then drive the picker over the corn and demonstrate what it would do. The farmer agreed and the demonstration took place.

To the amazement of the farmer the picker picked up every ear of corn except one. He immediately called this one ear to the attention of the salesman who proposed they go look at the missed ear of corn. They walked to the ear and the salesman picked it up and showed it to the farmer.

"No wonder it wouldn't pick it up," he said. "It's MOLDY."

By the time of the Arab oil embargo of the 1970s, we, like most farmers, had transitioned to combines and drying system. By 1978, I was faced with the fact of higher drying costs and the fact that I had a very good ear corn crib and a 237 John Deere picker, so I decided to buy a two-cylinder tractor to put the picker on and leave it on.

My local JD dealer told me I was in luck. He just happened to have a 1949 G that my brother-in-law had traded in. It had great rubber, new batteries, and was only $550. Dang! He forgot to tell me that no John-Deere-mounted picker would fit on a G. They are just too wide across the block.

A little measuring disclosed that all of the extra width is on the right hand, or clutch side, of the engine. I moved the picker lift arm an inch to the right on the picker sub frame. Moved the picker axle mount one-and-a-half inches to the right. My local machinist turned a spacer one-and-a-half inches thick, which I placed between the hub and the wheel on the right hand rear wheel, moving that wheel to the right.

With the addition of an air cleaner, we had a one-of-a-kind 237-ear corn picker on a G John Deere. We used it for several years. Both the picker and the G are still in the family.

3

When Getting "Wired" Meant Just That
aka
The Gold Medallion Outhouse

Guarding the Path

The year was 1939, the depression seemed to be ending and WWII was a horrible possibility in the not-too-far-distant future. F.D. Roosevelt had decided it was time to bring light to rural America. Every rural area was in the process of forming, or had already formed, an R.E.A. R.E.A. was New Deal terminology for the Rural Electrification Administration. Local co-operatives were set up and, with federal assistance, brought light where there had been none.

One requirement was that all farms in an area had to agree to use the services. The process was underway in our neighborhood. The only possible problem could be one next-door neighbor who had an excellent thirty-two-volt power plant, powered by wind, with an auxiliary gasoline-powered generator.

Dad opted to wire the house. He also bought a new Frigidaire, and the nicest radio anyone ever saw. Dad liked radios. He hired the top—and only—electrician in town. Everything had wires strung to it. The garage, the granary, the three barns all had two new copper wires going to them. Then came the surprise. The two wires also went from a switch by the rear door of our house to the outhouse out back.

You may have guessed by now that the neighbor with the light plant wouldn't agree to use the R.E.A. services. He stalled and the other neighbors fumed. When Pearl Harbor Day came, Dad improvised. He traded the Frigidaire (for the duration) to a friend who had electricity, for a refrigerator that ran on kerosene. He bought an old engine-powered milking machine that also lit a six-volt light bulb while he was milking. We still had a good battery-powered radio on which listen to the "news." "News" consisted of how the war effort was going. The trip out back was still endured in the dark, rain or shine, hot or cold.

Then came the glorious day. The war was won. Automobiles were being built. There were tires, gasoline, and sugar for consumers. One could actually order items from the Sears Roebuck and Montgomery Ward catalogs, which, of necessity, eventually made their way to the building out back.

Finally, after all these years, there was light. They hooked up the lights. There were lights everywhere on the farm, including the outhouse. Winter approached and it became apparent that Dad's dream from years ago was not yet to be fulfilled. He was obviously looking for something which only he had envisioned. Finally, he found it. He came home with a brand new twelve-inch, free-standing, adjustable, electric radiant heater.

We were instructed on how to place the heater, pointing it at the seat, each time we left the facility. The next trip, one only had to flip the switch by the back door and, depending on lead time, upon your arrival the seat was warm.

We were also warned that if we left it pointed at the Sears catalog, we very likely would burn down the place. Mother seemed to worry more about that contingency than we boys.

This arrangement lasted for another three years when running water arrived in our home, along with it a stool that flushed.

I know I can't prove it. But I do firmly believe that our family had the first, perhaps the only, all-electric Gold Medallion outhouse.

4

Random Threshing Memories

Threshing scene circa 1917

WAGONS

The racks in which the bundles were hauled were usually seven feet wide by fourteen feet long. The boards on the floor of the rack were placed with a space between each board. The space is a half-inch, perhaps an inch, wide. The floor certainly would not hold water. In the center in the front of the rack was a standard. A standard looked very much like a five-foot-high ladder that was integral to the rack. A frame, perhaps two-feet high, surrounded the floor like a short wooden fence. That was called the "basket." Mention was made in my brother's writing of a place in the rotation at the machine. The bundle haulers were expected to follow the same person to the machine with each load all day long. Everyone hauled the same number of loads in a day. The first one to the machine to start the day was the first one to go home in the evening. One could not violate that without being ostracized by the others. Hay/bundle racks were also used by farmers to haul loose hay to their barns. Each farmer seemed to create a rack that fit his ambition quotient. Some farmers made their racks eight-by-sixteen feet with a high standard, others made their rack six-by-twelve. They might hold their place in the rotation, but they did not all make the same contribution.

These racks sat on four wheeled running gears. They were constructed with a heavy wooden beam for an axle with a steel wheel on each end. The front axle pivoted about a pin located in the center of the axle. That allowed turning. During a turn one wheel was moved to the front as the other moved to the rear. (Much like children's coaster wagons today.) A very sharp turn reduced stability because the wheels were no longer across the load. The front axle was fastened to the rear by a "reach"; a reach was a two-by-four usually of hickory. The above-mentioned sharp turn could, and frequently did, break the two by four reach. This break effectively disconnected the front wheels from the rear. Breaking the reach was not looked upon with grace. By the time I joined the crew these wagons were being pulled with tractors. Frequently these wagons still had the tongues in them that were meant for horses. That placed the ten-year-old tractor driver some twelve feet in front of the front wheels of the wagon. Driving on a bundle wagon was an honor for a ten-year-old. Errors were not well accepted by the owners of the equipment.

THE MACHINE

Belting up. A threshing machine is comprised of various components that move in different directions at different speeds. A flat belt drove each component. The belts were not "endless"; they were spliced canvas belts. The splicing was accomplished by clamping a series of metal clips on the ends of the belt. When the ends of the belt were brought together a steel pin was pushed through the metal clips. It held the belt together. At the end of every work day the belts were removed, rolled and placed inside the machine. That protected the canvas from the weather. Two belts were difficult to remove so they remained partially in place. The main drive belt that came from the tractor to the machine was rolled up on built-in mechanism. The belt that ran the weigher was captured at the top end by support arms, so it was removed from the bottom pulley and just hung there. At the beginning of the day, the first order of business was to "belt up." Every belt was a different length and different width. Some belts ran in a figure eight or crossed configuration, others did not. Not belting up correctly would result in some components running in the wrong direction.

The machine was always belted up to move. If a move was made with the belts rolled up and riding on the inside of the machine there was a high probability that the pins holding the belts together would shake out. There are two basics that are essential to the proper functioning of the machine: (1) it had to be level and (2) the speed of rotation of the input shaft had to be correct. In thresher jargon that speed of rotation was called "motion." There were many other variables. The amount of air moved by the cleaning fan could be varied to meet special crop conditions. The common term for this was "wind." The variable that was out of control of the machine man was the flow of bundles riding on the feeder slats into the machine. There was a direct correlation between the uniformity of this flow and the consistent cleanness of the oats going out of the separator. Too many bundles going in would cause machine speed to slow. That would trigger a governor, which stopped the feeder. When machine speed recovered the feeder would begin to move again. Young men, pitching into a machine that was marginally powered, would delight in stopping the feeder. More frequently the cause of consternation for the machine man was inconsistent feeding. One of our neighbors had an ability to be standing on every bundle that he was going to pitch into the machine. He would have to move before placing each bundle in the feeder. Others could make it look as if it were choreographed.

DRINKING WATER

The water was on site. It was pumped from the well in the morning and went to the threshing site on the first bundle wagon. It was contained in a ten-gallon galvanized cream can. This can was placed on the shady site of one of the rear wheels of the tractor that was furnishing power to the machine. The water would be exceedingly warm and frequently have a faint taste that indicated the can had cream in it recently.

ACCIDENTS

As already mentioned, there was a tremendous opportunity for accidents when threshing. In the early days of threshing bundles were hauled from shocks in the field and stacked in large round stacks that were placed at the site where the machine would be placed. This allowed a longer season for threshing in the days of steam when there were more farms and fewer separators. Dad told the story of a steamer pulling on site, losing control, and running into the stack of tinder dry oats. If one thinks of a steam engine as a portable fire, it points out the problem. Unfortunately, I don't remember the rest of the story. I suspect that if something had burned I would remember it.

The following account is one that I observed from start to finish. I would have been a teenager when this happened.

I was on site one day when Dad was still the "tractor man." He insisted that there was a state law dating back to steamers that required a man at the machine and one at the tractor. They were to be in those positions whenever they were threshing. He was never far from the tractor and could frequently be seen just sitting on it observing what was happening. Dad liked to have the least possible tension on the 120-foot drive belt that it was possible to have and not slip. This belt was one that ran in the crossed, or figure-8, configuration. When it was run loose and under power the belt would cross very close to the tractor and far from the machine. On this particular occasion Arnold Dunn was pitching into the machine from the belt side. He missed the feeder with one bundle and it fell on the belt. His reaction was to reach for it with his fork rather than let it fall to the ground. (It was not good form to leave bundles on the ground when you drove away.) Because of his hasty effort to salvage the bundle Arnold fell from the bundle rack onto the belt, which would start to carry him one way and the return portion would catch him and take him the other way. Dad was on the tractor seat and it seemed as if he reacted before Arnold hit the belt. The belt would have been traveling at 3,100 feet per minute. Arnold would have been traveling downward sixteen-and-a-half feet per second. He had only about three or four feet to fall, so I'm sure that he was on the belt before it began to slow. One motion disengaged the hand clutch and engaged a pulley brake that was not designed to stop a threshing machine in an instant. Dad threw the full weight of his body into the clutch lever. The machine stopped quickly. Arnold rolled off the belt onto the ground got back on the wagon and Dad restarted the machine. I do not recall anyone even discussing the incident.

5

Threshing, the End of the Story

What an interesting challenge. This trilogy was begun by an ageless aunt we call Aunt Honey. Aunt Honey is the richest person I have met. She is rich because of her values, not because of any worldly wealth. She is a good storyteller, too.

My brother, William F. Probert, supplies the second part. He is also a very good storyteller. It fascinates me that Florence T. King, aka Aunt Honey, recalls the beginning of threshing "rings." Recollections of threshing rings before the rapid decline in the number of truly family farms are supplied my brother W.F. Probert. In his experience bundle wagons still had steel wheels and were pulled by horses. Although I am only some twenty-five years younger than my aunt I saw the demise of threshing as a way of life.

The person with primary responsibility for the death of the threshing ring in our community was a neighbor who farmed 110 acres. In our neighborhood that was not a very big farm. On any given year, he would be tilling less than 40 acres. He pulled the neighborhood into twentieth-century grain harvesting. He accomplished this feat with a 1934 open fan shaft Model A John Deere tractor pulling a 12a John Deere combine. No loud whistle. No smoke. No parade of neighbors with their wagons. He could harvest his oat crop in one day. All of those days that had been spent threshing at other farms could be spent as a custom oat harvester. He was fed well at those farms too. He was leading a revolution. (He would hate that statement.) That period of time was the beginning of tremendous change.

Some mention has been made of the reason for an oat harvest. Oats were horse feed and people feed. The straw was needed for livestock bedding in the facilities in use at that time. I have seen harvest numbers that indicate the largest total yields were during Abraham Lincoln's administration. Horses were the power source and hay and oats were the power fuel. W.F. mentions seeing the last draft horse leave the farm. In a sense, a lot of oats were replaced with the oil flowing from the ground.

My experience with a real threshing ring lasted perhaps six years. Our father purchased a Minneapolis Moline Combine in 1939/40. It was purchased from Pixler Implement in West Union. Dad used this machine for four seasons. It was not a good experience. For the threshing season in 1945, he bought an International 28-inch machine. That meant that the spike-tooth threshing cylinder was 28 inches long. He purchased it from the Leahy brothers of Wadena. The drive pulley diameter dictated that it be pulled with a Farmall tractor. Since pulleys were not available because of WWII, the people who had been furnishing the power came with the machine. Bert Erickson and his sons Bill and John were farming the Leahy farm east of Wadena. This farm was also known as "the Brick." The Ericksons were one of the lucky few families that were able to obtain a new tractor during the war. They had a "wartime" International Harvester Farmall M. Also in the package were the services of machine man Alfred Johnston. He was a neighbor and longtime friend of Dad's. Soon a John Deere was powering the machine. Serious changes began to take place in the summer of 1951. Alfred, the machine man died that year. Dad had just purchased three new John Deere Tractors. The largest of these, the Model A, was to supply the belt power. It was decided that I would be the "tractor man" and he would become the "machine man." My few seasons of driving on the bundle wagons ended. By 1954, ours was the only farm in the ring. Oat acres had shrunk on our place from eighty acres each year to twenty. That year Dad, our hired man, Arnold Dunn, and I did it all. Dad and Arnold cut the oats and I shocked them. They would come out each day and cut what I could shock. Arnold and I loaded the bundle wagons, unloaded the bundle wagons, and took care of the grain. A neighbor, Glen Probert, baled the straw pile.

An era ended.

6

Land of Milk and Honey

When the feed bunk is never empty
And the stock tank is never dry.
When the silage never freezes
And the calves always come feet first.

When the line fences never need mending
And the creek fences don't wash out.
When the banker asks, "Are you going to need more money?"
Then I will know I'm in the land of milk and honey.

7

Fifty Years of Progress

The guy at the Land Bank said I'd never make it. He said I'd never make money as a farmer or cattle feeder, that I was just a speculator.

I kept telling him that wasn't so, those cattle will make money this year—or sooner, or later. It all came from the highest finished cattle-market in the history of the free world. Too bad our local banker cut off our open-ended cattle loan back in '79.

If he had just stuck with me for twenty-five more years—what glory would have been mine. After all, we made money back in '66. They should have known everything would be fine.

Unfortunately, I can't tell the banker "I told you so"; sometime back in the '90s he left for greener pastures.

It has been hard to accumulate a large number of cattle on my wife's retirement. She honestly thinks there are better places to invest it. It only adds to the tension when I purchase cattle feed with my old-age pension.

I suppose I would be pushing my luck if I started talking about a new one-ton diesel truck.

It would be hard to justify one without attaching a twenty-five-foot aluminum trailer to it. Wouldn't that be a sight to behold? I'm just sure the banker would say, "You're getting too dang Old."

Hope springs eternal they say. It's sure enough true with an Iowa cattleman, or he wouldn't make it through the day. Certainly those thirty head of cattle I sold on markets like that could justify the purchase of a new cowboy hat.

8

Wintering One Hundred Head of Steers—Silage

"The eye of the Master fattens the cattle" Scottish Proverb

Here in Iowa
We were unique among our peers.
The only fools in the county
Who tried to winter a hundred steers.
Weighed a thousand pounds,
Grass-cattle, thin at the ribs,
And straight in the rounds.
Pasture all summer,
Cornstalks in the fall.
When winter came

They were six feet tall.
When snow came
Winter them we would.
I guess the reason was
We did it because we could.
Corn silage and hay
The best we could get
Put the hay up dry
The silage wet.
The first cold spell didn't matter
Silage came out nice.
That second cold snap got us
The silage turned to ice.
The silo looked like a committee designed it.
They wanted volume all right,
But they seemed to a have a penchant
For width over height.
It was strange looking
Even in our state.
The diameter was twenty-four feet
The height twenty-eight.
You might as well work alone
It was too cold to talk.
Every trip to the far side of the silo
Was a forty-eight-foot walk.
That walk was bad enough
No one called it nice.
It all got compounded though
After the silage turned to ice.
We did things right,
We were no one's fools.
A pick, an axe, and sledgehammer
Were the necessary tools.
With pick and axe, we would work.
Output slowed to a trickle.
What eventually took shape?
We had carved out a fifty pound popsicle!
Ten more minutes,
We usually calculated,

Swinging the sledgehammer
Would make it granulated.
There remained one more
Problem in store,
How to get the silage particles
Twenty feet to the door.
As usually happened
With the passing of time
We'd get enough silage out
To start feeding down the line.
Said to be a bushel basket,
That was quite a laugh;
Printed right on the side
It said a bushel and a half.
The feed bunks were with the cattle,
They were scattered at large.
When you carried the first basket
A hundred steers would charge.
The way to carry a basket,
If it is cold or even colder,
You just boost it up there
And carry it on you shoulder.
A hundred head!
How they can push and shove!
I wouldn't try that now
For money or for love.
Fifty trips would do it
Slow or fast.
It made one appreciate
Last summer's grass.
We always started silage feeding
Very early in the day
There was still water to open
And then feed the hay.

9

Wintering 100 Head of Steers—Water

Another part of
Wintering one hundred head of cattle
Would be impossible for a wild-west cowboy
To do from his saddle.
We had to feed them,
But maybe even worse,
When they finished eating,
We had to quench their thirst.
We called it a "crick."
Some might say a small stream.
Getting water from it
Was a nightmare instead of a dream.
It was spring-fed all right,
That was really neat,
Eighty rods downstream
That spring water lost all its heat.
That little stream
Obeyed all natural law.
It expanded when froze
Stayed that way—until it thawed.
Somehow it could expand
With banks on each side.
Several days of 20 below
And it's 40 feet wide.
Sometimes
Like magic in the night
It would overflow and freeze,
To a remarkable height.
Innocents the first time
We went down there
On a seemingly hopeless quest for water
Our question was, "Where."
It was always there
Waiting to be found
In that little space
Between the ice and the ground.

Take an axe and start chipping,
Not just anywhere,
Not without looking, maybe signs
Of yesterday's hole are there.
On those days when
Water ran over the ice and froze
It added to the depth
An amazing growth.
It was a beautiful thing
Clean fresh ice in the morning light
Laying there glistening for miles
Like a horizontal stalagmite.
You could chop for an hour
Trying to find the hole.
One doesn't sweat much
When it's 20 below.
Sooner or later.
We weren't allowed to quit.
We would finally make
The decisive hit.
The water built up pressure
Between the ground and the ice
When one broke thru to yesterday's hole
For a moment the water would squirt like a geyser.
It's hard to explain
The negative satisfaction
Of a totally freezing water drenching
After an hour physical action.
When water strikes clothing
Or skin when it's 20 below.
It's instant ice
Nothing about it is slow.
We didn't seem to mind it.
It happened every day.
A slap and a shake
It disappeared like cubes from a tray.
We had water for a hundred steers.
It worked out just fine.
They would all drink from the hole
One head at a time.

10

Winter 100 Head of Steers—Mud

The third part of the wintering trilogy
Is a different thing.
It doesn't come till later,
In Iowa, we call it "spring."
The silage thaws,
The crick melts and floods.
We turn our earflaps up,
The feedlot turns to mud.
There is some gear we wear,
It's certainly nothing new,
We wore it all winter,
The five-buckle overshoe.
We still carry silage
In a basket on our shoulder.
After all this winter watching
The steers know the order.
What has changed now,
What lessens the thud,
When those steers hit us

We land in fourteen inches of mud.
Feet stuck in the mud,
Bunted by a steer—full grown,
One tends to bend and sway
Like a human metronome.
Basket in balance
You continue to sway.
If you don't land in the mud
You count it a good day.
The moving is slow,
You made it this time.
The remaining trips
Now number forty-nine.
One thing in common
For which we all strive
Is for the 100 steers and us
To reach summer alive.
As with all happenings
There is an end to it all.
We'll grain them this summer
And sell them in the fall.

11

Ode to a Hole in the Ground
or
All Is Well

It is not my place to sound the alarm
But by the grace of God
We sold the farm,
Bunches of money, for pieces of sod.

Hilly as Scotland, wet as Wales
Punctuated with rocks,
Inhabited by creatures with no tails,
And natives with no socks.

I survey the scene as a whole
As I look around.
I realize the place met its goal
It filled a hole in the ground.

1 2

Ghosts

Your head is on the pillow
There's a rhythmic booming in your ear.
It could be your pulse surging, or
It could be the ghost, of a two-cylinder John Deere.

You're standing in your yard
On a day that's crystal clear.
That could be a neighbor plowing in the distance, or
It could be the ghost, of a two-cylinder John Deere.

The clouds are black, thick as diesel smoke,
And thunder rolls draw near.
Tell the kids, "That's Grandpa and Jesus"
With a two-cylinder John Deere!!!

Don't worry, children, never feel bad,
They are warming it up, to show it to their Dad.

1 3

It's Storming Today

It's storming today.
How long will it last?
How will it compare
With the storms of the past?
It is hard to believe,
Looking off to the east,
In a day or two
It will all be at peace.
How many inches will fall?

What about the wind chill factor?
Will drifts be impassable?
Can we get out with a tractor?
Winter storms with their trouble and strife
Leave a lot fewer scars than the storms of life.

14

Life in the Margin

There was no long-term plan.
I was just being me, I meant no one harm,
I just had an earnest desire.
All I ever wanted to do was farm.
They changed the darn rules
Between then and now,
Though it worked fine for 10,000 years
It has almost become illegal to plow.
The soil is kept out of sight
On today's technological trail,
Primary tillage appears to be accomplished
Pulling a rooster by the tail.
Now they call us marginal farmers,
A new term in this new age.
We get the margin
The big guys get the page.

15

What's in the Attic?

The story begins, I fear,
With slight distress to the ear.
It ends later, as the noise in the attic grows
Greatly affecting the nose.
My parents were concerned, I recall,
With loud nighttime noise in the walls.

The battle began. Dad was on the attack.
He was after rats or mice. He was on the wrong track.

He became adamant as the noises persisted.
It must be a squirrel. He then insisted.

A trap in the attic; that should work.
The plan was followed by nature's quirk.
A ladder in the hallway through a crawl hole in the ceiling.
He fastened the trap securely. Surely we'd have the thing in the morning.

We all awoke really quite early.
Our attitudes were bad, dispositions surly.
That squirrel—the one in the trap
Turned out to be a civet cat.

The difference is plain to those who knew,
A skunk has one strip, a civet cat two.
One can't imagine, nor even think
How one little animal can make such a stink.

The thing was alive. But it really was sore.
Its stomach was empty as was its reservoir.
We'll climb up the ladder, stick our head in to see.
Suddenly, I realized—the "we" meant me.

The plan unfolded. Just cut loose the chain,
Pull it out, drop it in a can.
Up the ladder I went, a very reluctant kid.
Dad stood there with a pail and a lid.

I raised the cover, put my head through the hole.
There two feet from my nose was the tail
Of a civet cat, blacker then coal.
As I started the task I began to realize
I couldn't do this, and close my eyes.

I gripped the chain with one hand, cast a downward glance
If I missed that pail there was no second chance.
I pulled on the chain, drug him down past my face.
One of us was about to fall from grace.

The animal flopped on its downward trail.
Whop! went the lid. He was alive in the pail.
The trip through the house just couldn't fail.
Dad and me and the thing in the pail.
The next few years were not a living heaven,
But the smell went away about 1967.

16

The Blacksmith

Before the dawn of the "throwaway day,"
"Design life" was not a common term.
Farm tools were built to last.
Blacksmiths built things, and they fixed them.

One of them came from Germany
Opened his doors and dared anyone to be better.
If you broke it, he could fix it.
Like generations before him, he took pride in his work.

He learned to fix things one at a time.
He finished, and then he moved to multiples.
While a plowshare heated to the right color,
One cooled and one was shaped with the hammer.

When the last piece of iron cooled,
When the last blow of the hammer fell,
When the forge grew cool cause no one banked it,
The door closed one day, and no one opened it.

It sat there in dust, dust from the street,
Dust from the feet, dust from the past.
It sat there waiting for the next generation.
The city preserved the site to help the memory last.

Unfortunately, the next generation works in
Courtrooms, operating rooms, and boardrooms.
Trained in wisdom and integrity by the Blacksmith,
The next generation will create a legacy of their own.

1 7

The Storm—Armistice Day

Everyone old enough,
Even those who were partly grown,
If they lived in Iowa,
They'll all remember the "Storm."
It is difficult for me
To remember the year.
I think it was 1940,
I know I was there.
Dad said we had a problem
We had to get the cows.
As bad as this storm is,
They can't stay on fall pasture now.
We all left together,
Including me, of course.
Dad, Arnold (the hired man), and my brother walked.
I was on a horse.
She wasn't just a horse.
She weighed more than a ton.
Her name was Susie.
My Dad trusted her with his son.
I was five and important,
She, bred to pull a plow.
We were quite a pair,
When I look back on it now.
I was kind of little.
She was fully grown.
We liked each other, we had a lot in common.
We were both pigeon-toed.
They left us there, old Susie and me,
To stand and watch a gate.
They'd look for the cows. We would wait.
It blew and stormed
On the boy and the horse.
We were all alone, but, all right, of course.
I didn't mind the cold
I had no fear,

Dad knew where I was, Susie was right here.
I don't remember the end.
I just remember the day.
Here is where he left us
Here is where we'd stay.

Susie and Jere

18

The Old Treadmill and the Horse Dan

(Written by Jere's Great Aunt Mary Jane Probert Borst)

The old treadmill was the bane of my life.
'Twas a thing of evil and harm.
It caused more emotions of fear and strife
than any machine of the farm.
The horses would shy with evident fright,
When they realized what would befall;
At the crack of a whip, they'd enter the fight
And climb to their place in the stall.
And when they were in, at the pull of a strap,
The wheels in motion would grind;
The nerve-racking noise of the run-away trap,
Would almost shatter one's mind.
With eyes staring wild, and nostrils wide,
The horses would climb and climb:
Their step carried them up, and on the endless tide;
No chance to rest for a time.
Among the horse clan, was one we called Dan.
Neither beauty nor speed he possessed;
Patience and care were both in his plane;
With good horse-sense he was blessed.
The good horse Dan, was a boon that is clear
As he climbed on his wearisome way.
Did he think, How queer! if he pulled the strap near,
For a much needed rest he could stay?
And then came a lull, no noise at the mill,
The floor stopped rolling beneath;
In Dan's head reigned reason and will.
For he held the strap in his teeth.

19

The Last Cow

Somebody raised such a fuss
About meat and fat and all.
I believe I wound up the owner
Of the world's last cow.

We ate her calves, drank her milk.
We've gotten by.
We thought we were stuck with each other,
That old cow and I.

The cattle sale barns all closed
As the modern thinking thrived.
Markets closed from lack of cattle,
Still, I kept that old cow alive.

We've grown old together
Mutual dislike increases.
There is no place to sell her
I guess I'll take her to a place for endangered species.

I push to load her,
She pushes back.
I push again—she voids
Her digestive tract.

We are chest to tail
When she decides to scoot.
My overalls are full,
So are my boots.

There must be someone to blame
For this mess all over me.
Am I the culprit or could it be
The cow, or perhaps, society????

20

The Contractor

He sits there, alone in his shop where he had worked on his equipment.
It was either there or in someone else's shop that his working days were spent.
The shop floor was swept, swept clean to his satisfaction.
Parts and tools are all in their assigned places, ready any moment to be called
into action.

The first sign of a good mechanic, they say, is a clean floor.
One can sweep and sweep and sweep some more.
The cataracts make it hard to be sure—any more.
It was quite a job to rebuild the shop after the fire.

It is good to not be too busy today; there is a little time to rest.
That old lawn chair the Missus threw away looks good
Right there
Where the Caterpillar always stood
For its winter tune-up and repair.

He is so glad that he put a stool and sink in the little side room.
A wood-burning stove almost keeps the old building warm.
You do need boots on a really cold day.
All those things give him a reason to come here
Just to be sure everything is okay and a chance to get away.

He thinks of winters past when he got the "7" ready to roll.
He brings his lunch
Just like he did when the shop was full.
You know, those aluminum thermoses really last;
He ran over this one with the Cat once.

No need to turn the lights on any more
Usually just sits after sweeping the floor.
The natural light is dim; the shop has long vague shadows,
The fire burns low as if it, like the light and the man,
Knows its job is nearly done.

Here he sits in the old lawn chair,
He leans back with his chin and his hands on his chest.
With his gaunt frame and full beard
He resembles nothing more than an old picture of a civil war veteran.
He rests his feet on a large wooden spool, now he's glad he didn't burn it.

In a quiet state of repose
Sometimes he contemplates, sometimes remembers,
Mostly he rests.
To God he says, "This is how I want them to find me someday,
When my day is finally done."

21

Whatever Happened to Wadena?

Occasionally, in the course of a conversation or exchange of information, a question is asked that is so simple that no one has a ready answer. It was a woman named Ruth who asked me that question. Her brother walked down a snow-covered Northeast Iowa dirt road in the early 1940's. He never looked back, he never came back, he never again contacted the family. He left at the other end of that road. He was wearing a US Army uniform when he left and Ruth decided to go with him. Eventually he abandoned Ruth, too. It was some sixty years later when Ruth asked, "Whatever Happened to Wadena?"

Watching a small town age for sixty years is a little like watching a person age. Suddenly there's gray hair, and you don't remember when it wasn't like that. I tried to recall what it was like so I could answer the question. Those memories came in no definable order. Certainly they didn't come in the order of importance, nor did they come in chronological order. I started to record the memories so I could make some sort of word picture of the metamorphous of the Wadena that Ruth and her brother walked away from so long ago.

One memory I'm sure she doesn't share is the smell of the men's outhouse in back of Heyer's Tavern. Even for a farm boy it was bad.

We often were in town on Wednesday and Saturday nights. People gathered there to "trade" at the grocery store. Eggs were brought in thirty dozen at a time and were candled immediately by the grocer to insure their freshness. A value was put on them, and the family went home with things that weren't on the farm—flour, overshoes, shoes, and clothing in whatever amount rationing allowed. Mother shopped while Dad and his closest friend, Mike, had one glass of beer, which they nursed for an incredible amount of time before going home.

The town put up a large billboard. It resembled the outdoor movie screens that would dot the countryside in a few years. They placed it in the vacant lot between Cooley's Grocery store and the telephone office. Ally Leonhart manned the switchboard. On that screen were the names of all the Wadena men and women who were serving in the War. It was pretty much filled with names and, as time went on, more and more of those names had a star placed by them.

Sometimes the star was blue, sometimes gold!

Ready to leave forever

There is an entry in my mother's five-year diary, August 5, 1945: "Dropped first Atomic bomb on Japan. Sister Ruth and nieces Bev and Lorraine found a ride to Iowa. Rained," August 22: "Arnolds went to fair today. Bill thrashed at Thore Thompsons. Leaving tomorrow for Shell Lake Wisconsin in morning. No gas rationing."

Suddenly, at least it seemed sudden to a ten-year-old, the town was filled with young men and women. The exuberance was tangible. Ruth and her brother were not in the crowd that came back. Many of those who had a star by their name didn't have a choice about coming back. Even Ruth's father, at age 44, had been drafted and served in the US Army for a time. He, however, came back.

Change came and came. There were new cars and new appliances and sugar and gasoline. There was a town baseball team. Every town had a team. Often the teams were staffed by returned veterans blended with the best of the high-school players, and the best of has-beens from an earlier era. Our team was playing every summer Sunday when it was fit to play.

Herwig's built a locker plant in the basement of the old opera house. For insulation, they packed the walls full of sawdust. Upstairs in the opera house, there were Wednesday movies and Saturday night dances. Either of those scheduled events might be followed by a street fight. The Fayette County Sheriff declined to come to Wadena on Saturday night.

There was Doctor Woods, the World War I, vet delivering babies and making house calls on frequently impassable roads. His pay was often in chickens and eggs. When a neighbor was killed in a buzz-saw accident, according to an eyewitness, they hauled him to town and laid his body on Dr. Woods' lawn for him to fix.

There were four churches to worship in. There were three grocery stores as well. There were four thriving taverns also. As if in one final effort to survive, the whole community pitched in to build a new gymnasium attached to the school.

Just as quickly as change came to Wadena, all of the exciting change left. It was replaced by negative change. The young men and women dispersed into the rest of the world the way a drop of water disappears on a sponge. They left for better jobs with higher wages. They left for college under the GI bill. Some just left. Unlike Ruth and her brother, most of these people would stop back periodically until there were no loved ones left to visit.

Then sadness set in. Old businesses closed. The grocery stores slowly and painfully went out of business. People took their new cars and drove to bigger towns where the variety was greater and the prices lower. The store owners aged and "new blood" could not prosper. Many of the better homes in Wadena were moved to those bigger towns as well. Prosperity seemed to have left town. One tavern survived. The blacksmith shop, the implement dealer, the filling stations, and the mechanics shop all closed. The Lutheran Church was moved out of town. The United Brethren was torn down and the Catholics closed their doors. That left just one eternally struggling church in Wadena. Farmers left their farms.

In 1958, the Wadena Independent School district gave up its independent status and merged with Elgin and Clermont districts. For a time, we had grades K through 8. Then it became K through 6 followed by K through 4. Then the Baptists from Volga purchased the school and used the facility for a Christian academy for many years.

There was an iron bridge that crossed the Volga River at the south end of Main Street. One day, like an exclamation point punctuating the demise of a town, the deck of the old iron bridge just fell in the river.

One of the men who had successfully left Wadena to seek his fortune came back. He invested some of his fortune in Wadena. Many of the families in town invested in the community. Their investments have been of time and talent as well as financial resources. Wadena has become a thriving bedroom town. It has a clean look. There are sewers and water and a couple of thriving enterprises. The old hotel has been restored into apartments, as have two of the old store buildings. Several new houses have been erected and several have been moved in from other sites. There are very few vacant lots in town. People with young children live in Wadena again. The ball diamond is well groomed and used for softball by all ages and genders. There is a convenience store, a library, a machine shop, and the locker plant still butchers livestock in the same facility with the sawdust insulated walls. There are no more regularly scheduled movies or dances.

In 1972, an event called "Galena in Wadena" happened. Promoters had advertised a rock concert that was to be held in Galena, IL. The promoters knew it would not be allowed in Galena because of the presence of illicit drugs and the other elements at rock concerts of the era. Using a form of "bait and switch" approach, the promoters purchased a farm just outside of town. Before authorities could respond, we had a three-day rock fest on our hands. It was estimated that more than 20,000 hippies descended on our town. The highway patrol, county, and local law enforcement set up headquarters in the gym, which had been built a few years earlier. After three days of sex, drugs, and skinny-dipping in the Volga River, everyone left town. Like Ruth, her brother, and the returned veterans from World War II, they went down the road with their backs toward town. They didn't look back, didn't come back.

SECTION II
Family

Back row: Jere and Beverly Probert
Front row: Children Lisa, Denise, Stephen

1

My Family

One thing I desire
One thing would make me glad
To be half the father
As the one I had.

It was the grace of God
As I look at life
That alone
Gave me this wife.

The Lord surveyed
His angel Pavilion
Picked three of his best
To be my children.

What more could a person be given
Than a loving family going to heaven.

2

Generation to Generation

Frequently, when asked to give an account for a specific happening, one must start somewhere else to make the happening more understandable. I have been asked to give an account concerning what was at the time an unusual spelling of my first name. Scottish tradition spells out very clearly the precedence of names in the family. First boy named after his father's father, first girl named after the mother's mother, etc. This results in a repetition of names that seems endless. But like the Unicorn not being in the Ark, there were no Jere(s) in the Proberts.

My brother, William F. Probert put together an excellent, comprehensive genealogical study of "our" limb of the family tree. I will borrow from that work but not attempt to duplicate any of it. My forte seems to lie more with the oral history genre. It leaves more room for interpretation.

In the early 1850s, our Welch-named great grandfather and his wife immigrated to the "New World" via Scotland. His brothers and sisters accompanied him, or he accompanied them, and they eventually settled in Highland Township, Clayton County, Iowa. There, for the most part, they established what appears to have been a close and prosperous community. Some of the Probert sisters married Duffs and inhabited the same hilly township as their brothers. Several other Scottish families lived in the same area, rounding out the enclave. This immigrant great-grandfather died very young. His widow not only survived on her own, she prospered as well. She and her youngest son James, aka J.C. Probert or Uncle Jim, put together a large—for the time—farm operation of some 960 acres in one unit. J.C., my father's uncle, eventually became owner of the land. He was fondly known to us as Uncle Jim, which is somewhat ironic since our father had a brother, James O. Probert (our uncle), who was known to us forever as J.O. Great-grandmother's will indicated that she possessed, at her time of death, considerable wealth, both land and cash.

Our grandfather, after some wanderlust, ended up raising his family on a farm near Wadena about five miles from the "home" place. He had four sons and two daughters. The oldest son was the above-mentioned J.O.

J.O. was considerably older than his siblings and reportedly was named after his uncle in response to a request accompanied with some cash. He married a local merchant's daughter and became the banker in Wadena. The other sons, Linn, Guy, and William V., remained bachelors for some time and farmed their dad's farm as the Probert Brothers.

Our mother moved to this community in 1922. Of German extraction, her aunt had married into one of the previously mentioned Duff families. In December of 1928, she married into the Probert family. She married William V. It is not hard to imagine, for the newlyweds, that it looked like clear sailing ahead. Some might even have said she married well. Her sister, Florence, talks about "the Probert money."

Several events happened very quickly after the wedding. October 1929 saw the stock market crash. Richard Probert, patriarch of this family, died, not quite free from debt. Dad's brothers, Guy and Linn, also got married, establishing new households that needed separate incomes as well. A son was born to William V. and Verneta on December 2, 1929. He was named William F. after his father and maternal grandfather. That would have been somewhat after the Scotch tradition. Suddenly, there were more mouths to feed and fewer resources to provide for them.

Remember J.O., the young banker, in the family? Well the banker, now my mother's brother-in-law was in a lot of trouble, because his bank was going under (being forced to close) and was taking community members' savings under with it. Uncle Jim's side of the family was told that all available money plus what could be borrowed against the home place was used to alleviate this situation.

In the first three years of their marriage, William and Verneta were "sold out" twice. Guy and Linn were farming with their respective in-laws. Our parents were farming as share-croppers (50/50 lease) on the recently mortgaged old home place for Uncle Jim. All three of the brothers appear to have entered into a sort of voluntary indentured servitude that was going to last the rest of their lives. J.O. ran a hog-buying station the rest of his career.

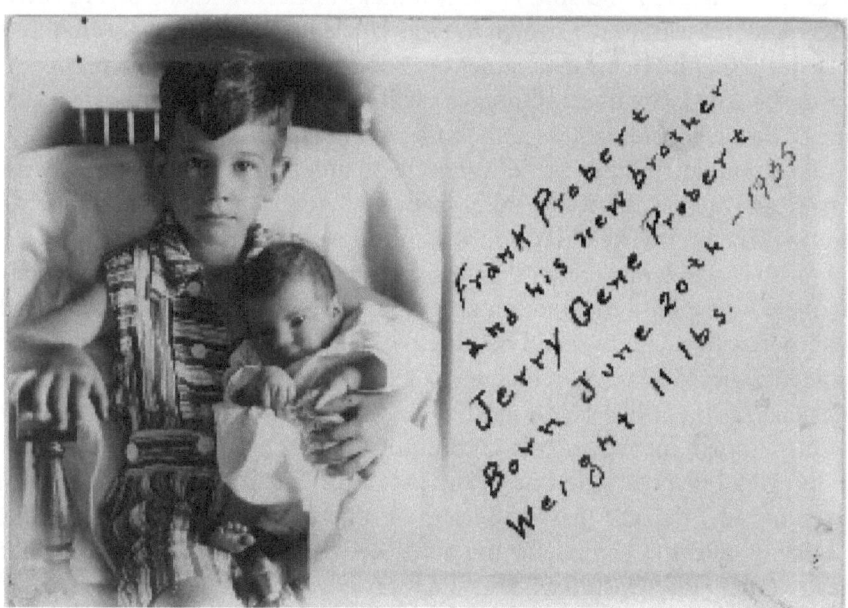

Baby Jerry (Jere) and big brother Frank

Now it is 1935, the heart of the great depression, and I am born. Another mouth to feed, I probably was supposed to have been a girl. Mother might have been a little disillusioned with the "marrying well" thing. She might not have been overjoyed that I weighed 11 pounds. I strongly suspect that it would not have been safe to suggest to my German mother at this point in her life that she should name me in the Scottish tradition.

They named me Jerry. I was born in Wadena, in the home of a practical nurse named Alva Clark. Her husband, Dawson, was a WW I vet who now did some photography.

For a birth announcement, Dawson was commissioned to take a picture of my brother William Frank holding me. Under the picture, which was postcard size, it said something like, "Frank Probert, holding his new brother Jerry Gene." By the time we were in our twenties, he was known as William or Bill and I had become Jere. That birth announcement was not helpful at all fifty years later when we were asked as a part of business deal to prove that we were brothers.

My parents were extremely permissive with me. I had wide latitude. In later years, as I was raising children, I became convinced that I was raised totally on faith; the let-him-go-he'll-turn-out-all-right kind of faith.

I was born with an extreme pigeon-towed condition. I could turn either foot inward until it was pointing back 180 degrees but could not point them beyond straight ahead. I never felt I received any special dispensation because of that defect. I was encouraged however to "explore." This was also a time when no little boys had toys, at least not in rural Wadena, Iowa.

When it came my time to attend the one-room country school, they had instituted kindergarten, or Primary, since kindergarten sounded like something Hitler would have in his dictatorship. One evening early that fall, I was sitting on a board gate to our barnyard during milking time and the rope holding the gate in place broke catching my leg between two boards and breaking the leg. The leg was set in Oelwein by an MD after being x-rayed by Dr. Olson, a dentist who happened to be the only one in town that night who knew how to run the x-ray machine. Since I had to walk to school, I missed a lot of days the first semester. At Christmas, I developed *Mastoiditis* and that grounded me for another six weeks. I Flunked Primary!

One thing I was supposed to be learning that year was to spell my name. I thought it sounded like Jere, and that is how I spelled it. Neither my parents nor the teacher attempted to correct me. I don't think this had as much to do with their permissiveness as it did with plain old pity for the pigeon-toed kid who couldn't pass Primary.

The subject of how my name was spelled was never raised again until I enlisted in the Army in 1956. By this time, I had enrolled at Iowa State College as Jere, had a checking account by Jere, and a Social Security Card issued to Jere. At least it didn't say in parenthesis (he flunked Primary).

To get this straightened up, I went to a lawyer who said the only way I could get it right was to file for a legal change of name. He charged me twenty dollars. He filled out the proper forms. I was to file them, and then had to wait thirty days and do something else with them. The waiting period, I was told, was to make sure I really wanted the new name. He told me you are only allowed one name change per lifetime. Before the thirty days were up, I was told by someone to just file a form claiming THEY spelled it wrong. Something felt very right about that so I used that no-cost procedure. So I really didn't give myself my first name, it was just that everyone else had spelled it wrong.

Almost exactly 150 years after my great-grandparents emigrated here from Scotland, I was living the same place they had lived and had my own name.

Interestingly enough, the only time I have had to produce a birth certificate was in 2004, when I applied for a passport in order to travel to Scotland. Until then, the only birth certificate I had was spelled Jerry.

3

When I Grow Up

When I grow up I want to be, clean and full and warm and free.
When I grow up I want to be, kind and gentle, big and strong, and free.
When I grow up I want to be, confident and challenged, seriously joyous, and free.
When I grow up I want to be right, righteous, loving and loved—and free.
When I grow up I want to be, husband, father, patriarch, and servant with integrity.
Like father, like son, I might be. That is okay, if I can be me.

4

Growing Up

When life was about growing up
Airplanes were flown by flyers
And the telephone worked
When it didn't rain on the wires.

Houses were homes
And children were
Not left there
Alone.

5

The Crooked Crowbar Stories

It was mentioned to me that some of my cousins, and perhaps some of their children, were lamenting the lack of any Probert family mementos. We would all like to have tangible items from the past. Unfortunately, there really aren't many "things" that I know about. I do have in my possession an old abstract that contains great-grandmother's last will and testament. It's interesting in the way she treated our grandfather. I also have a little notebook which our great-grandfather used to record some formulas for making iron and steel. I would be glad to have them copied for anyone who wants them.

In lieu of any objects from the past, I do have a "Roots" type story which I would like to write for posterity. Unfortunately, there are side stories that go with it, and I'm not ready to record them all yet. One is about "Uncle Billy" the pyromaniac, his encounters with his sister, and his trips back and forth to Scotland. Other anecdotes include why Richard and Mary chose to farm at all and why they chose Northeast Iowa. His final illness and death at a young age is another topic as is his frequent migration back to Pittsburgh to work. Mary's personality, education and management ability are legendary as well. There are also "The Blau Eirie" and "Uncle Jim's Breaking Horses" stories. Those are some of the stories I have heard and think could be accurately retold.

The story I want to tell is not only about remembering stories but also about my finding out the accuracy of one of them. I sincerely doubt that it has been embellished in the retelling over the years. Before I tell the story, which I call the "Crowbar Story," I need to identify a few characters:

THE SCOTTISH IMMIGRANTS, CARLUKE, SCOTLAND

Richard Probert	Iron worker, Mary's husband
Mary Longmuir Probert	Wife, mother, farm entrepreneur

ONE OF THEIR CHLDREN

Richard Probert	lumber worker, farmer Lucy's husband
Lucy Kimball Probert	died young

THEIR CHILDREN

James, Mary, Linn, Guy, William V., & Georganna

THEIR CHILDREN

James	son of James
Jeanne	daughter of Linn
Marion and Leland	children of Guy
William F. and Jere	children of William V.

One soon realizes, upon examination of the Probert family tree, that those of us who are not called Richard, William, James, or Mary, probably weren't priority Proberts.

Early in the decade of the 1850's, Richard, the immigrant, brought his wife (Mary Longmuir) to a parcel of land on the border of Fayette and Clayton counties in Iowa. She eventually farmed 960 acres, mostly in section 19, Highland township, Clayton County, while he worked in the steel mills in Pittsburgh (that is another story). He did return to Iowa on occasion, at considerable effort when one considers the transportation available at the time.

Before one of his trips back to Iowa, Great-Grandfather Richard decided to fabricate a crowbar to bring to Iowa for use on the farm. It seems, upon packing for the trip, that he found that his newly manufactured bar would not fit in his trunk, it was too long. He decided that the most practical way to solve the problem was to heat the bar, bend it double, carry it to Iowa, reheat it, straighten it, and temper it at his destination. Upon his arrival in Iowa, though, he found that there were not adequate facilities to create enough heat to perfectly straighten the bar, and it was left for eternity with a very perceptible S curve at the point where the bend had been.

I recall hearing this story repeated several times during my formative years. It was usually told when Linn, Guy, and W.V. Probert were together. The story always ended something like this, "I wonder whatever happened to that bar? It was still around when we were kids, you could see the place where he bent it and couldn't get it straight again."

Some years ago, I was attending a livestock auction in Wadena when a lifelong acquaintance of mine, and a relative of all us cousins, came in and sat next to me. He started a conversation by saying, "You know, I have something that came from your farm."

"You do," I replied, "what is it?"

"A crowbar," he said. "When dad came to this country, he worked on that farm a few years and when he left to go on his own, he felt the place owed him something, so he took along an old crowbar."

I said, "Does it have a bend in the middle?"

He looked astonished. "Yes, but I don't know how it ever got bent; two men can pry on it and not straighten it."

The acquaintance was Robert Longmuir of Arlington, Iowa. Robert was the son of Alan. Alan had emigrated in the early 1900s when that bar was forty to fifty years old. He had worked on his aunt's farm to get a start.

Robert told me he had given the bar to his son who is farming northeast of Arlington.

Robert Longmuir and the Crooked Crowbar

6

Talking Crowbars

Excerpts from an Email to Cousin Marlene Noble

I received your letter today. I am honored by your request that I record some family stories on an audio cassette. Having been informed of your various activities I was surprised to hear from you. I hope you would not be offended if I would prefer to write the stories rather than put them on tape. I have written a lot of "stuff" since those items I sent you from ten years ago. Some of my family members have copies of everything I've written. By writing rather than recording these stories they can easily be added to that collection. My mind seems to go into a blank condition when I am confronted by an open mike, so this will be easier for me as well.

You asked for clarification about when our grandfather returned to Iowa from his west coast adventures. The story I was told said he was brought back because of rumors of an eminent catholic-protestant war, to fight if needed. I would guess this was prior to 1901.

Our Uncle James Oscar told of seeing his grandmother Mary grab her brother Billy by his scruffy beard and "read him the riot act." Uncle Billy seemed to have his name on several significant parcels of land in Fayette & Clayton Co. We only knew of 40 acres adjoining Mary's until Frank began his family tree work. It, believe or not, was called "Uncle Billy's 40." We found that he was an early landowner of several hundred acres. I don't recall ever hearing of him being active in the daily routine work of the farm. A speculator?

As you stand with your back to our mailbox Blauwerie is a quarter of a mile to your left (north), the east side is marked by the road upon which you are standing. Another quarter mile to the north and west puts you on the first land he purchased. Yes, you are facing the building site that was located at the base of the hill.

You pose an interesting question about Alan Longmuir's relationship with Mary Longmuir Probert. I just took it on faith that he was Mary's nephew. If indeed he was a nephew he would have had to be a younger child of a younger brother of hers. I make that deduction because of his relative age. He was much closer to our father's age than our grandfather's age. He was another potential source of information, with which I did not confer.

We do have a picture of his son holding the famous crowbar.

I hope you will ask my brother for a copy of his transcript of the 1902 diary of Rob Duff when he worked here. It is a good look at the work and in my mind an amazingly socially active life. There is a record of his taking a train from Volga, Iowa, to South Dakota. He left Volga on Thursday, traveled to South Dakota, looked at a piece of land, and was back in Volga for a basket social on Monday night. There are accounts of frequent neighborhood baseball games and other social activities.

You also asked about any accounts of music in the first generation. I have no memory of any accounts of music in the Probert house. All the talent during the time I can remember was in my Uncle Guy's family. He, his children, and his grandchildren were all blessed with talent.

Jere

7

Some Memories—Widow Probert

The story that I was told about why the Probert family was drawn to settle in Northeast Iowa was that it looked very much like the land they had left—except that there were vast hardwood forests here. There was (is) abundance of water flowing year around, flowing from springs into spring-fed streams. Abundant water, water that never freezes even when it is a minus 40F. For a family who were to become livestock farmers it was all they could hope to find.

Viewed from today's perspective one would wonder why they chose to settle where they did. They traveled westward for several miles, from the Mississippi River, across prime farmland known as the Garnavillo Prairies. They stopped traveling west twenty miles short of the beginning of the finest farmland in the world. They stopped in cattle country. Having reviewed all the research that crosses my desk about the family, I wonder if they were the stereotypical "penniless immigrants." It would appear that they were counter-revolutionaries during the industrial revolution. Generations previous were apparently spent in the iron business. Now the Proberts as well as the Duffs, Kerrs, Pollocks and Medberrys came to be farmers.

The appearance, in my opinion, is that Richard and Mary were more in the category of land speculators than farmers of the era. People who wanted a family farm settled on 40, 80, or perhaps 120 acres. That was all a family could run. Many 80s or 120s that were settled in the 1850s supported a family—including the building of a nice set of farm buildings and a home. That is what many of the families listed above did, as well as immigrants from other European countries. It seems to me that Richard and Mary wanted to do more than make a living farming. A supporting anecdote is that several of the old farmers who were alive when I was starting to farm referred to the place as "the ranch." As in someone saying to me, "Granddad used to tell about hunting rattlesnakes on the Probert ranch." It is almost unheard of for a parcel of land east of the Missouri River to be called a ranch.

The old timers told us that Great Grandfather became ill on the farm while they were still living in the log cabin by the stream. My recollection is of being told that it was some sort of stomach-related ailment (appendix was speculated). Whatever the ailment, a person was dispatched to get a doctor from McGregor, Iowa. That person was sent some thirty-five miles on horseback and returned with a doctor. Obviously, since this trip would have taken three or four days, he was dead by the time the doctor arrived. We were also told that one of the last things that Richard and Mary L. Probert did before this illness was to decide where the buildings for their farmstead were to be built.

By 1869, she had completed construction of a large T-shaped house, which is the home my brother and I were raised in. The home was largely constructed of native lumber. One account told of the Township Trustees coming to see the Widow and offering her a pension or some sort of monetary relief since she had lost her husband. She reportedly physically removed them from the premises.

Another family story related that Mary L. Probert was barely literate. More precisely, that story said she could write her name, and that was about it. One of her "sayings" that lasted and impacted long after her death was, "the Proberts would have an 'eddication.'" College education for all seemed to end, according to family legend, after Linn Probert was involved in a "blowing up" of a chemistry lab at a small Iowa college where he was a student. To my knowledge all children earned twelfth grade diplomas even if they had to reside in a different town to find a four-year high school. As for Mary L. Probert's family, not only did they get an education, but she saw to it that at least two of her daughters were highly educated. One with a Master's from Upper Iowa in the 1880s.

In 1877, the railroad had penetrated to within three miles of the farm. This is the same period of time when the forests of northern Wisconsin and Minnesota were being harvested. These huge trees were made into log rafts and floated down the Mississippi river. Sawmills were set up along the river, the logs were sawed, the lumber shipped by rail to inland farms. Grandmother's first "real" barn was constructed of this material in 1878. It was the "cow barn," as opposed to the "horse" and "steer" barns. It appears, from our perspective, that she liked "big" things. This first barn was about forty-by-sixty feet with a twenty-four-foot beam. That is, twenty-four feet from the sill on the basement to the plate on the roof. Sixteen feet was the standard for that distance.

The barn sat on a native limestone foundation eight feet tall. It was said that they mined enough limestone to fill a basement and then they used it all to lay up the walls. They were three-feet thick, chinked with lime. It was nearly fifty feet from the ground to the peak of the roof on the south end. "Uncle" John Probert Duff told of an itinerant standing at the end of a ladder, painting that peak, while singing "May the Circle be Unbroken." That struck Uncle John's sense of humor. The pine beams in the barn, some of which were eight-by-eight inch, forty feet long, and some twelve-by-twelve by forty feet were without knot or blemish. This barn became a history lesson in itself. The practice was for anyone who worked there to leave at least their initials carved in the soft pine. Frequently there were messages or statements carved in the wood. Things like harvest dates and little personal insults between the men were carved in it. One inscription that I recall said, "1933 & 34 two years in Hell."

The horse barn was built in 1887. It was constructed of the same material but even more solidly. This barn had the stall space for twenty-two horses. This at a time when no farms had a separate barn for their work horses, and few farms would have had even eight work horses. The rock walls on this building were closer to ten feet high to provide clearance for the horses. It had a built-in bin for oats, a large hay loft and a corn crib just outside.

By 1912, a Steer Barn, ninety-by-thirty-six feet and a hog house a hundred-by-eighteen rounded out the livestock buildings. Those are all big dimensions for the era. The construction of the later buildings was not as classical as the early buildings. By 2001, none of the buildings were left standing. A classic Midwestern tornado that occurred Memorial Day weekend 1985 completely destroyed the two oldest barns. During the 1990s, the steer barn fell victim to a collapsed foundation; and in the year 1999, the current owner destroyed the home.

Some Personal Observations—as if the rest of this were completely objective??? Growing up on the Probert farm as William V. Probert's son and William Frank Probert's brother was a challenge for me. There was, for me, a sense of pride in being related to those two, but an awareness of the expectations the community seemed to have for any with our name. Visiting Uncle Jim's (James C. Probert) in West Union was, for me, a terrifying experience as a little boy. The only option open there seemed to be good behavior—very good behavior.

A personal note on the education story, I often joke that the only time our father told me what I should do was when I did not want his opinion. If I asked his help he would answer with a question. When he was in the hospital during his final illness in 1969, he told me there were three things he wanted me to do. (1) quit smoking, (2) sell the farm, and (3) finish getting my BA (go back to college).

8

By Request

I have a request to document the three stories enclosed. I think that when this type of story needs my documentation its origin is highly suspect. What I can affirm is that these are stories that I have heard, or think I have heard.

The first account finds me at odds with my brother about details. I will call your attention to those discrepancies in *HIS* story as I get to them.

There was a time of development in the ongoing agricultural revolution when whole corn plants were harvested for livestock feed. They were harvested with an implement called a "binder." They were packed into bundles that were processed. One process was to set the bundles up in groups called "shocks." This was done after ears were set but before the corn plants matured and dried. These shocks were left in the field until totally dry. They were then hauled to the farm site where the bundles were run though a machine called a "shredder." Each bundle was fed into the shredder by hand. The shredder removed the ears from the stalks, tore up (shredded) the stalks and blew them out the back of the machine into a pile, usually in a barn, as well has having just the ears harvested for feed.

My account is that the man who rode (operated) the binder had trouble keeping his glove on one hand. It seems that when he performed a particular function involving his hand, the binder grabbed his glove, removed it from his hand and destroyed it. The solution was obvious after the third lost glove. He proceeded to put on his glove and tied it on his hand with twine from the binder. The next time he performed the previously mentioned task the binder left his glove on his hand and removed the hand. *My brother's account is the same, except his story has him feeding the shredder instead of the binder. Incidentally, his story has the person losing his arm instead of his hand.*

Somewhat less bloody is the account of the Kimball Brothers, possibly great uncles of mine. They owned a threshing machine and the steam engine that pulled it. The traction steam engine was used not only for belt power to drive the machine while it was threshing, it was also used to pull the machine from one site to another. In this day when we think of towing equipment we see the use of a ball and socket. However, that's not the way it was done then. The tractor doing the pulling has a steel drawbar with a hole through it. The implement being pulled has a "tongue." The tongue has two steel plates bolted to it. These plates protrude beyond the end of the tongue. These plates have holes in them that must be aligned with the hole in the drawbar of the towing vehicle. A steel bolt, called a "draw pin," is dropped through the aligned holes and away you go. Steam-driven tractors, when moving from the stopped position, moved in rather large increments—perhaps several inches per "jump" would be a conservative estimate. To move slowly and in small increments the engineer would leave the steam shut off and turn the flywheel by hand.

It seems that the day of the incident with the Kimball brothers one of them chose to use his finger to align the holes while the other one chose to use steam as a method of propulsion. The resulting amputation was instantaneous.

Our father, who was born in '01 (the other '01) told a story about twin boys that grew up in Wadena. The twins, by his account, were not what are generally thought of as model citizens. Not even in Wadena. As I recall hearing this story it seems to me that they must have been older than Dad yet young enough that he could give this first-hand account. It seems that these twin boys, or young men, had been given nicknames. The residents of the town knew them as Nit and Nat. If some one told a more "for sure" account of their names I would gladly concede. It seems they lived in a house close to the center of Wadena, right along the west side of Main Street. (This was the home, I think, that was later occupied by Mayor L. Knox and his wife Marj. Marj later wrote many historic accounts for local publications.)

It seems that Nit and Nat would occasionally get drunk and get in fights (with each other). Usually the site for the fight was the front lawn of the house. This far into the story there is not much unique about it. The part of the story that transforms it into something I have remembered is the weapons they allegedly used to fight. According to Dad they used broad-axes as weapons of choice. I understand that broad-axes may have been a weapon of war in the middle ages. By the twentieth century they were pretty much relegated to the more mundane life of being used to fell trees and shape logs. Except, that is, in Wadena, Iowa, in the hands of Nit and Nat.

I just finished this story and have a PS for it. I received a call from my brother stating that there were twins named Leo and Leon, slightly older than our dad. Leo lived in Wadena and I knew him. My brother stated that Nit and Nat had a relative who ran a tavern at the south end of Main Street. He also told me that the house I described above was owned by relative of theirs and was a tavern and boarding house.

9

Sonnet to a Gray Hair

In 1989 our oldest daughter discovered her first gray hair. She removed the offending hair and taped it to a sheet of black paper and mailed it to us with this note.

"*Dear Dad and Mom,*
  "*You saw my first steps, you were there the first time I fell down, and you saw me off on my first day of school. You were with me through many of the firsts in my life. I thought you would want to experience my first gray hair as well.*"

The following verses are my response to that letter.

It's a trustworthy observation
That nothing can compare
In the process of aging
With finding the first gray hair.

Harder still to believe
That no one else has a care
About the color
Of that one little hair.

We are sure that for you
It is a time for great sadness
Certainly not rejoicing

Or gladness.
But that gray hair you took the trouble to save us
Is *not* the first one you gave us!"

When she received my response our daughter put a copy of both letters, along with a cover letter, and mailed it all to the *Readers Digest*. They published it in the June 1989 issue, at the bottom of page 128.

10

10

Appreciation Day

(In honor of my mother-in-law, Reta, a summary of my thoughts about the mother of my wife.)

You are an ongoing gift.
A gift to our life that refuses to be measured by value or years.
You are the one who always brought something to the table.
Yes, you brought food
and all of life's staples.
Those things have been great,
Prepared with love and served with Grace.
We, in your community, know you served us with a lot more.
You made every effort to meet our needs from your bountiful store.
You minister to all as you see their needs.
When we need to grow, you plant the seeds.
Through broken promises, broken hearts, and broken hips,
You continue to serve others and soften the way on their life's trip.
And all we can manage to say is
Thank you and we love you on Reta Appreciation Day.

11

HOLDING HANDS

(Father-in-law's Death, for Reta)

He first held your hand a long time ago.
When you were so coy.
From deep within you
You're heart burst with joy.
Then there was that day
He gave away the bride.
He sat and held your hand.
Your heart burst with pride.
When you were burdened,
You sat and you cried.
He held your hand.
You were satisfied.

Too soon came the day,
The gift from above,
He took your hand dying,
And your heart burst with love.

12

Fourteen Lines to Beverly

(During '80s farm crisis—why we made it.)

I appreciate your notes
When life really stinks.
They keep me afloat.
They never let me sink.
When my nose is in the ground
Your love is always near.
I just need to look around.
Your presence always brings me cheer.
Love is your specialty.
Even with your tears.
Having you next to me
Helps my sky to clear.

13

Thirty-Eight Years

Thirty-eight years of
Fun and trouble and love,
Growing and flowing.
Flowing together not drifting apart.
With eternity ahead,
I've just gotten a start
With you.
I'm thankful for today.
I'm thankful for the past.
I'm looking forward to tomorrow
With joy and not sorrow
With you.

14

On Being Inadequate

Once again today,
I need to take the time to say
How much more you deserve
Than one with only half a heart to serve.
Because of you, I have joy in the Lord.
I look forward to the Kingdom we're moving toward.
You nurtured love from my inner soul.
He has used you to make me whole.
As the winter of life draws near,
You are a constant reminder there's nothing to fear.
The love I have for you transcends knowing
It just keeps on growing, growing, and growing.

15

God Did a Special Thing

God did a special thing when He created you.
He did another special thing when He decided to
allow me to spend my life with you.
You are a light shining on so many—in the school,
in the church, and in the family.
I know of no one who shows more of the attributes
of God, the manifestation of the Spirit than you.
God reveals Himself to me through you every day.
I am proud to say on the correct February day that,
"She's my Valentine."
I love you,
Have a Great day.

Beverly Probert

16

Valentine for That Favorite Person of Mine

I know that it has been awhile
Since I told you how I enjoy your smile.
I wonder if it is your little quirks
That help make this marriage work.

The finger pointed for punctuation.
"How was your day?" as salutation.
Having the courage
To turn that handle away when I ladle porridge.
The "upbeat" attitude
When I'm out of fortitude.
You're a woman of prayer
When I'm not there.
Those times, when one way or another
You work in, "You act like you mother."
The great haste with which you flee
When confronted by a bee.
The quirk that gets my attention without fail
Is the weekly trimming of the toenail.
I don't want you to think the list is short
I'll put the rest in my next report.
Lest you missed the point this time
I want you for my valentine.

I love you,
Jere.

17

Blondes

"Blondes have more fun,"
It is said in jest.
Having one for a wife
Is by far the best.

18

Miss You

I miss you today
Too cold to play
Too wet to hay
I miss you anyway.

When I'm down,
You lift me up.
When you're gone,
I'm in a rut.
I love you,

19

On Romance

There is a time to be romantic.
It should say that in the Bible.
I am sure it could be there as well.
That there is a time to be Contrite.
Like changing the clocks in the spring and fall.
Romance requires action with discipline and
It seems to be at least one day too late
When I finally get it right.

20

Friday Night Date

School is fun.
Farming is great.
I'm looking forward
To our Friday night date.
I love you.

21

Proposition or Proposal?

When it's all done
When the battle is over
How about a frolic in the clover?
I love you.

2 2

I Love You, Bev

I love you.
Please don't be sick.
You're the only true friend
I've had.
I love you.
Please don't be sick.
It makes me sad.
If only I could change it quickly!

2 3

Who Cares

Who cares about syntax
Words, and such.
All I know is that
I love you so much.

2 4

Nice Person

You're a nice person.
Everyone seems to know it.
This must be a reason
Your countenance shows it.
"I'm the Lucky One"

2 5

My Saintly Norwegian

For priests and nuns
And other, to celibacy drone.
I much prefer my saintly Norwegian,
Who knows where she's goin'.

26

Kissing

We hardly deserve an x-rating,
But we've been kissing since we've been dating.
Now for a suitable conclusion,
Is this for real or is it a delusion?

27

As Long As You Are Near
I Don't Care Where You Are

I look around and you aren't there.
I do what I do as if you were here,
Or very near.
And then I pause and look for your smile.
Listen for your laugh, then I look around.
You're not there.
If this were a test, I doubt I'd pass.
A test to see how long I'd last,
How well I'd survive
Without you.
It is a struggle to know you're not in the other room.
It is a relief to know you're on your way, you'll
Be home soon.
If this were a test to see how I'd do without you.
A trial run to see how I'd survive or if I could,
Perhaps I would
For awhile.
I could survive with no joy in being alive.
There would be no reason left to laugh
Perhaps I could
Without a smile.

2 8

My Most Favorite Person

She's always there
Seven day a week.
She's forty-four without a care
And still hasn't reached her peak.
After twenty-five years
Of wedded bliss,
Not many tears and
Always a kiss.
Complete with hair of red,
Of her ancestors she's proud.
Until the day she's dead
She'll stand out in any crowd.
She's filled with love and thrift,
Straight from the Lord, a delightful gift.

2 9

Christmas is Coming

Christmas is coming
To my delight.
Can't wait to unwrap my
Present on Christmas night.
Have you taken the
Time to notice, I suppose,
That neat leads to sweet
And all of that to repose.
We've had lots of growth
Since you became my little girl.
None at all though in the
Areas critical.

3 0

Christmas 2000

(for my Beverly)

Here we are at the end of another year.
The very front end of 2001 is nearly here.
We've had a good year, sometimes we would even listen
And sometimes responded to the prompting of His Spirit.
Is it difficult to be of good cheer?
When we look out the window, there is a definite glisten.
The South Dakota Spruce so full of snow they look like snowmen.
I look at you and give thanks. For I know in my heart this
Christmas *must* be the best that has ever been—for you and for me.
Together we shall celebrate and be thankful.
For the gift God gave to us, the One He allowed to be hung on a tree.
I alone shall celebrate and be thankful for His other gift.
The gift God gave, when He gave you to me.

3 1

Community Service

The noise you hear
Is just to let you know
That once again
The old Frigidaire is on the go.
The meeting was long
It wasn't a blast.
But I still give thanks,
It wasn't my last.
I'm glad the car's fixed
And I'll be more prudent.
After all,
I'm still a student.
Tuesday's are long,
And they get so draggy.
By tomorrow night my
Eyes will be baggy.

All of this is to say
Without any jest,
I love you so much.
You are the best.

32

Twenty-Seven Years

Twenty-seven years,
Isn't that astounding?
In spite of our fears,
Isn't love still abounding?
I have had so many "ups" with you
And so very few worries.
There have been lots of "I love you"
And not much need for "I'm sorry."
The years have gone by
With extraordinary speed.
Like the passing of a sigh
Or a tree dropping its seed.
There is still as much love, or maybe even more,
As there was the last year or any before.

33

To Bev at Forty-Four

Happy Birthday!
Now you reached the age of forty and four.
Everyone will wish for you to have a great many more,
Till you're sick to death of the silly show.
This fact is forevermore.
From me to you
That one forty-four
Beats two twenty-twos.

Thanks for the joy.
Thanks for the pearls.

Thanks for the boy.
Thanks for the girls.

You are the head of the class.
You are five courses with pie.
Not a whole lot of sass,
And basically shy.

The consensus among men,
Without a doubt all agree,
Because I heard it again:
There is a lot of leg below the knee.

You taught me to love,
Me, the unreachable.
When a Jesus' love
Finally made me teachable.

You know we are one
Through His strength so mighty.
Don't worry, Hon,
Together we're over ninety.

34

On Love That's Aged for Thirty Years

Some things in life are hard to explain.
There are droughts, and luck, and rain
And pain
And love that aged for thirty years.
There are things that grow
With time and care
Or things that get fine,
Like wine
And love that's aged for thirty years.
For us there's been
Little sadness.
Joy,
Two girls, a boy

And love that's aged for thirty years.
Sometimes
The future may seem
Shorter than the past
But we know it's meant to last.
Love that's aged thirty years.

3 5

Elisabeth

(Our oldest granddaughter)

To start at the start, she was a skinny baby,
Long, red, and slippery so they said.
She had some areas that were slightly rusted,
But, Who Cared?

It was in the Lord we trusted.
With all of that and an attitude,
She didn't allow Mom and Dad much
In terms of latitude.
But, Who Cared?

With the Lord's help, they adjusted.
She started looking good,
Appeared to be a candidate for Hollywood,
The rest of her grew long and willowy,
That just left the attitude.
But Who Cared?

With the Lord's Help, She adjusted.
Now high school's ended, she's made a graceful exit.
From her, what else would one have expected?
If there are any "BUTS" left,
Who cares??
She Graduated!!!!!

3 6

Traits
On Being Able to See, to Touch, to Measure, to Weigh

(For William Frank Probert's 75th Birthday)

If I were to select the traits I would put in a brother
If I were the one who could pattern the design,
I would pick and choose those traits I most admire in another.
I would look for things that he could adjust and refine.
My brother would be able to take traits that seem mechanical,
To see, to touch, to measure and to weigh.
My brother would take them and make them practical.
He would enjoy his uniqueness each day.
He would be able to *see* that roots and relationships create a platform for
launching.
He would be able to *touch* lives with humor and compassion.
He would rejoice in the trajectory of the lives around him.
He would love in *his* fashion.
He would take the *measure* of the world around him and then improve it.
Each change would be for the better as if responding to some divine sequence.
He would have the ability to *weigh* the inherent value of human character,
Fragilities and strengths. With grace he would accept the difference.
Lastly, to my delight he would have great genes and a memory
So we could continue to tell stories and call it a great beginning rather than
Three Quarters of a Century

3 7

It Wasn't All Roses

(For in-laws fiftieth wedding anniversary)

Seven hungry children
With lots of runny noses.
You got them thru childhood,
But it wasn't all roses.
Then there were school days
With "I don't knows" and "I supposes."

You saw them graduate,
But it wasn't all roses.
The weddings started happening,
Happiness and pain in large doses.
A son in the war,
It wasn't all roses!
We love you so much and pray,
As the door of this day closes,
That all your memories of it
Are only of roses!

38

Some Folks

Some folks can take a weed,
A dandelion,
And turn it into sparkling golden wine.
Some folks can take a tree,
A willow,
And turn it into a cradle with a warm blanket and pillow.
Some folks can take a glass,
A sparkling crystal,
and propose a toast that blesses one and all.
Some folks can take the sun,
The moon
And see nothing but good now with more coming soon.
Some folks can take a walk,
A stroll down the street,
See the whole world and declare it to be great.
Some folks can take a nap and dream
Dreams that make their troubles flee
And awake refreshed, full of glee.
Some folks can take a risk,
A leap of faith, a chance,
And reap a lifetime full of love and romance.
Some folks can take a day
Full of fog or freezing rain
And see something too beautiful to explain.
I can take a look and see you

Like new, as if for the first time,
And I'll tell the world I'm glad your mine.
You can take a day,
Any day, any time,
And you can be my Valentine.
I love you

39

Sometimes I Think

I think sometimes in the quiet of the night,
A little boy during the war and the strife,
I'll be all right as long as Dad's alive.
I think sometimes in the quiet of the night.

I think sometimes in the quiet of the night,
A farmer, a father, two little girls are my delight.
Will they be all right as long as their Dad's alive?
I think sometimes in the quiet of the night.

I think sometimes in the quiet of the night,
There's a son now, I'm much older, farming's a disaster.
Will he be all right as long as his Dad's alive?
I think sometimes in the quite of the night.

I think sometimes in the quiet of the night,
My wife lies beside me, I hear her breathe,
It stirs my soul, like leaves in a breeze.
I'll be all right as long as she's alive.
Sometimes in the quiet of the night
If that breath doesn't come, if I lost her.
Forever alone, I'd not be all right.
Sometimes I write, in the quiet of the night.

40

Softness

Horses can gently nuzzle.
They have softness in their muzzle.
There is something for the whole world to gain
In the softness of an early spring rain.
There is softness in a favorite pillow.
In hot chocolate, there's marshmallow.
For some, there's softness, I'll bet
In the radiant colors of a summer sunset.
Two with softness blest,
Are the baby at mother's breast.
There is nothing in the world softer
Than a father's heart, touched by his daughter.

41

When Paths Cross

Today was the day
A baby died.
He never had a chance to grow.
He never lied.

His time was short,
So much he missed.
He hardly stayed
For a good-bye kiss.

The short time he was here
His path crossed with others.
The message he left
Was to love one another.

We all wonder, why.
Why was he so fragile?
Not at all what we expect
When God sends an angel.

42

The Pigs Are Out

"The pigs are out," he said.
It was his final vision, from his last bed.
"They are all over the side hill, tearing up the grass."
He was not sure he saw them, or if this sight would last.

"What should we do?" I asked, his hand firmly in mine.
"Should we get them now? Or should we wait a time?"
He struggled to think for a moment before he replied.
"Let them go," he said. "We couldn't get them back now, even if we tried."

On a better day he said, "That old man in the next bed? Rutherford's his name.
Ninety-four years old. Wife died a year ago. He says he'll never be the same.
He spent his life with the railroad. Supervised the laying of track.
He says he came here from home to die, and he isn't turning back."

"Try to get him to talk to you, he knows things you don't.
Some days he'll talk a lot, some days he won't.
Just listen to his words, an educated man, pay attention to how he talks.
His favorite things are railroad stories, and taking long lonesome walks."

"There is that young guy in the other bed. George is his name.
He lost three fingers today in a corn picker; ran them through a chain.
He thinks he is going home tomorrow, but he is still pretty pale.
By this time tomorrow, he'll be glad to stay here awhile."

We each paused, in silence, for a little rest. To visit a private sorrow.
He, drifting away from a life well spent. Me, sadly facing tomorrow.
Deep within us, we both knew our ways were parting.
Way too early, it seemed to me, our days together should just be starting.

It is getting harder to swallow now, the food goes down so slow.
Sometimes it takes a lot of coaxing, to overcome his "no."
The oxygen is irritating, the IV aggravating, the atmosphere degrading.
This experience is not one of hoping, waiting, only hopeless anticipating.
I didn't know how to say "I love you," I wouldn't even try,
Almost just as tragic, I couldn't say "Goodbye."

43

Letter to the School Board

March 26, 1990

Dear Dr.

I need to write to you to express a couple of strong emotions which I now harbor. I hope you will see fit to share them with the board of directors, your Special Education director, and the appropriate people within his division.

Members of the board may recall my advocacy of a suicide prevention program a few years ago. When the dust settled around that issue, we were implementing a crisis intervention activity instead. Having never been even remotely affected by a suicide, my position at the time was purely intellectual rather than experiential. It seemed to me that the first responsibility of an educator should be to do whatever is necessary to keep the student alive. It also seemed to me that your agency was better equipped by mandate, inclination, and ability to provide quality leadership in that arena than any other entity. Since suicide is a cause of death that is theoretically 100 percent preventable, it made sense to me to try to prevent the act rather than to minister to survivors as crisis intervention does.

Recently a very close friend of mine, a sixteen-year-old girl, and a student in your educational area, attempted to end her life. As a result of having observed and experienced the trauma that the event generated, I would like to urge you to give further consideration to a program aimed solely at suicide prevention. Only you at your agency have the opportunity to impact nearly 50,000 K-12 students in Northeast Iowa with one program. Rest assured that I do understand the need to prioritize based upon budget and personnel limitations within the agency. Please consider it again. What deserves a higher priority than a human life?

The family of the young lady asked me to be a part of the experience during the first forty-eight hours after the act. I contacted the appropriate agency people, they were compassionate, knowledgeable, and helped me in every possible way to say and do the right things during that critical time. I want to thank each of them. As we looked into post-intensive treatment, the agency was again understanding and helpful—thanks. In this situation, it seemed to be important that people cared. The people I contacted at your agency cared.

Thank you all,
Jere Probert

44

109 Sunset Street

Just over the top of the hill on Sunset Street,
The first home on the West of the crest,
Perfectly named and perfectly placed
For this last day of November, Sunset now passed.
Winter darkness, cold and thick, had settled in the night.
The visitor, aware of all the symbolism, stood for a moment
And appreciated the faint glow of light that seemed hardly
Bright enough to make its way through the window pane.
One slight push on the doorbell button
Brought the man—the son—to the door.
His immediate response was,
"Mom, we have company."

Having spent a few days at the local hospital
They left there without regret.
Mom and son had decided she would spend her last days at home, 109 Sunset.
They were now two days into her journey from Sunset Street to Glory,
She lay unresponsive on the living room couch.
There were long moments of silence as long as the shadows in the darkened
room.
Silence that was broken only by the bubbling of the oxygen generator,
And the faint sound of oxygen escaping around her nose.
He held himself proudly, treating her with indescribable respect.
A son, a man, keeping the family integrity intact.

They had lived as mother and son alone together.
The specter of death could not, would not change that.
He had a book given to him by the visiting nurse.
The nurse had been there yesterday.
This day, the last day of November, no one came.
No one was called.
The book had a page with symptoms when two or three months remain,
A page with symptoms displayed when only days are left,
And a page when minutes or seconds are left.
"The days and nights are long and lonely," he said.
"But now we are on the last page."

In his late sixties, most of his adult life had been spent meeting Mom's needs.
Since Dad died, they were a common sight
At church suppers, the doctor's office, or courthouses in three states.
As his interest in genealogy led them.
The visitor stood there watching the events of the last page unfold.
He cherished the gift of being a privileged witness,
A witness of a special private time.
A time of beautiful, raw emotions and love untold.
In his spirit the visitor thought he could hear Mom say,
as God once said,
"This is my son with whom I am well pleased."
As son ministered to every need, a servant's heart was on display.
The visitor excused himself
And he left 109 Sunset,
Understanding that the beauty of a sunrise can be matched
By the beauty of the sunset.

45

When Families Malfunction

When a family malfunctions
It can't be fixed by huggin and kissin.
Screamin won't help, neither will hittin
Or so it appears from where I am sittin.

There are better ways is my lamentation
To practice the art of communication.
It would surely help, is my supposition
If one would talk—and one would listen.

Section III
Faith

I HAVE MET
THE
MESSIAH

HE SAVES   HE HEALS   HE DELIVERS

AND

HE ISN'T ME

1

Faith

Faith is to be acted on.
Faith is a gift God gives so we can receive His Son.
Faith acted on produces Supernatural results.
Faith not acted on produces none.

2

What Is Praise?

I wonder Lord, just what is Praise?
What is it that honors you?
Should we lift our voice, or our hands be raised?
Or will our heart attitude do?

3

Praise

Lord, I Praise You.
With my innermost being, I praise You.
All of my days, I will praise You,
My soul praises You.
You are my Hope.

4

Met the Messiah
Devotion 1995

"But seek ye first His Kingdom and His Righteousness; and all these things shall be added to you. (Matthew: 6-33, *New American Standard*.)

We farmers tend to see our identity from a different perspective than people in other occupations. This identity has been adopted by society and the term "family farm" is a result of this perspective. It implies that the majority of our worth to society derives from our ability to produce something in the agricultural realm.

Each challenge to the farm operation is a threat to the identity of the family. Under this threat we prioritize accordingly. If it is planting season or harvest, it is the most important event. Therefore, it seems, the farmer's first love is the land. It is the very source of the family structure. The second love, then, is the livestock. Unfortunately, under this system of prioritization, family relationships, personal health, and safety are less important issues. The farmer often views his/her spirituality as derived from his/her occupation. In this system a relationship with God through Jesus Christ with its promise of guidance for today is not on the list.

Prayer for the day. Dear God, today I pray for these farmers. I pray that they may see themselves as you see them. I pray that they see that they are important to you no matter what degree of earthly success they may achieve. May an awareness of your love engulf them during this season. In Jesus name, Amen.

5

Law of Love

LOVE GIVEN AWAY IS NOT

A DECREASING

THING.

IT

GROWS

AND GROWS IN

AN EVER—INCREASING RING.

6

Trust

Why do we humans think
We need to explain
The stars, the sun, the moon,
And the rain?
Why do we humans think
We need to explain
Each joy of life, each change,
And the pain?
Why is it so easy to blame God
For the pains inflicted,
When we are the ones who should
be convicted?
Does our need to explain spring from failure to trust
In the grace of God through Jesus, given to us?

7

TWO EGGS
TOAST AND SAUSAGE

Once upon a time a noted theologian was invited to a prayer breakfast in a town where he had just relocated. Typically, theologians are not breakfast people. It seems that they do their best theologizing late at night, and breakfasts being a morning thing it is not a meal they enjoy or care to partake of. He did, however, think that under the circumstances it was in his best interest to attend at least once. Obviously, he would have to delve into this so he would not seem out of place. He had asked the person what would be served at breakfast and was told that since the meeting was held in a restaurant he could order whatever he wanted. Word study seemed in order.

Researching eggs became a nightmare. Imagine his confusion when he found that almost everything on earth lays eggs. One will certainly have to be more specific than to just order eggs. After all, the finest scholars say that there is a tremendous variation in size between—say—ostrich and fish eggs. It will be important, according to the earliest writing on the subject, to order chicken eggs. What a surprise to find that chicken eggs and humans are alike. It doesn't make any difference what color they are on the outside, they are all the same on the inside. It should be acceptable to order chicken eggs. There was that one section on nutrition, though, which implied that more than four egg yokes a week could be hazardous to your health. Maybe two would be the right number. He also found in his research that eggs were often served in combination with toast and something like ham, sausage, or bacon.

The word search on those three revealed that their earliest origin did not appear in the Hebrew community, which cast doubt on their authenticity. As a matter of fact, most of the reason they were developed was as an effort to extend the length of time they were edible. Hardly a hearty endorsement in the 1990s.

At long last the dreaded morning arrived. He forced himself from bed, not recognizing how lucky he was to be a theologian. They all have beards, so at least he didn't have to shave. He arrived at the restaurant, being the third one to arrive. It became apparent early in their sharing that the first gentleman was a Calvinist, the second an Armenian.

After a brief period in which no one else showed up they asked the waitress to bring them the menu. They surveyed the menu and the Calvinist, who was the first to order, said "God is sovereign; therefore, what 'I' want is subject to His will. What I will get is preordained anyway."

The waitress gave him one of those breakfast shift looks and said, "What do YOU want"? Sensing that she might not be following his line of reasoning he responded, "Just have the cooks surprise me." He was trusting that God would work His divine will through the cook.

The Armenian was next and he told her, "I really don't feel worthy of anything, I am such a sinner; it is only by His Grace that I am here. Do you suppose a glass of orange juice would be asking too much? I really don't deserve any more than that."

The withering look from the waitress said, *I'll bet they don't tip either.*

As his turn came, our long-suffering hero gave his order. "I have devoted much prayer and study to this," he said. "I will have two eggs, sausage and toast. I am not really comfortable with that, but it will do until I have time to look into this in depth."

Instead of leaving the table, to his surprise the waitress started to ask him questions. "How do you want your eggs? What kind of toast? Patty or link?" He then engaged her in a philosophical discussion on the relative merits of each possibility until he was thoroughly confused, as was she. He ended up ordering a sausage omelet with one slice of each kind of toast. Just as this transaction was closing, a member of the store-front congregation across the street joined them. He glanced at the menu and said "I'll have the special."

In the passage of time the Armenian was served first. His glass of water on the table was soon matched by one of orange juice. The cook sent the Calvinist a veggie burger and a glass of milk. She had peeked out to look at him and thought he looked like maybe he had an ulcer. The waitress brought the theologian his toast and omelet. He waited impatiently for the last delivery to see what such an impertinent order as "the special" would bring. He was amazed to see two eggs, over easy, white toast, and a sausage patty. Upon seeing it he knew that was what he had been desirous of at the start. "How did you get that?" he asked.

The reply, "Because the menu listed this as the special and I have a personal relationship with the cook, we've been friends for years, she knows what I want before I even ask."

8

Confession

Dear God,
I have failed as a father,
But you have not failed me,
For you have been a parent
To me and to my children.
I have failed as a husband,
But you have not failed me.
You have nurtured and blessed my wife.
You have been her lover.
I have failed as a brother,
But you have not failed me.
You adopted me and made me a brother to many.
You guided me as a loving older brother.
I have failed as a farmer,
But you have not failed me.
You created in me a new heart.
You have made me a fisher of men.

9

Neighbors and Friends

God created marvelous things in the universe,
The sun, the moon, and the stars.
We see them for a lifetime.
He created them, just for us.
Then comes a long, cloudy, rainy day.
We miss that sunshine. The sky becomes dreary gray.
Sometimes that day is followed by a starless night.
We begin to question, "Was there ever any light?"
God created more things in the life of man.
He created things we call neighbors and friends.
Like the sun and the stars,
We take for granted that they will always be ours.
Then for a brief time, the friend, the neighbor is out of sight.
Once again, we ask ourselves, "Will there ever be light."
In this moment, it is memories we ponder and enjoy.
Memories of hard work, fun and a man who could tell a good story.
From here we can see the line fence.
For generations, it marked a boundary, a point of reference.
A line fence doesn't separate neighbor and friends.
It is the place where they join in a cycle that never ends.
So we pause, give thanks, then we repeat it again,
Thanks that Floyd Thompson was our neighbor and friend.

10

Another Confession

I failed as a friend,
You befriended me.

I have been sick,
You healed me.

I have been dull of mind,
You gave me your wisdom and knowledge.

Jere Probert

My heart was empty,
You filled it with love.

My spirit was dead,
You resurrected it with life and power.

I have been weak,
You made it my strength.

I have sinned,
You forgave.

Rich is Your kingdom.
Great is Your name.
Blessed is Your Son.
Powerful is Your Spirit.

11

A New Budding Relationship

A

NEW

BUDDING

RELATIONSHIP

WITH CHRIST IS A

MORE PERMANENT AND

BEAUTIFUL THING TO SEE

THAN

A

TREE

1 2

Always Unfinished; or, I've Looked

(After three years employment at West Union Implement)

Lord, where is the man so profound?
I've looked and I've looked.
He is nowhere to be found.
I've looked.

Where is that man so wise,
With ideals so high
And a penchant for surprise?
I've looked.

Lord where is that man with lofty goals
Who cared for all
And loved their souls?
I've looked.

Lord where is the man whose hopes
Wouldn't die.
Who always said, "No goal is too high?"
I've looked.

Has he lost his way?
Only you know for sure,
I would venture to say.
But I've looked.

Just what were the causes?
Was it too much sorrow?
Too many losses.
I've looked.

I know the chances are slim,
But can You bring him back?
I sure miss him.
I've looked.

Maybe his goals weren't pure,
But his heart was right.
There were things about him I liked for sure.
And I've looked.

I think you are responsible.
Have you recycled him?
Is that possible
I've looked!

We'll recognize loved ones in Heaven it is said.
Why can't I recognize me now?
Will I when I'm dead?
I'll look.

13

C
H
R
I
S
T
DIED UPON A CROSS
F
O
R

T
H
E

L
O
S
T

C
H
R
I
S
T
DIED ONCE UPON A TREE
F
O
R

Y
O
U

&

M
E

14

Questions and Answers

There is a question we should ask every day.
There is an answer that changed the world in every way.

An answer that gives us hope when we pray.
There was a Friday when it became night in the day.

It was followed by THE Sunday when they asked,
"Who rolled the Stone away?"

15

Love That Aged

The love that led Jesus to the grave
Was about thirty years of age.
So I thank Him daily with tears
For a love that aged for thirty years.

16

Cowboys and Preachers

(A Sonnet for Charlie)

Have you ever wondered, my friend,
Why cowboys tend to prattle?
To understand completely
Just spend ten hours in a saddle.

Cowboys haven't found
What preachers so easily find.
Too much time on your rear
Dramatically affects one's mind.

Good preachers preach short and to the point.
Good cowboys ride for work and for sport.

No matter how long the journey
They say it was too short.

To think they have nothing in common is totally absurd.
They are both committed to every critter in the herd.

17

God Will Make a Way

God will make a way
where there seems to be no way.
He works in ways we cannot see.
He will make a way for me.
He will be my guide,
hold me closely to His side
with help and strength
for each new day.
He will make a way.
He will make a way.

18

Greatness

Greatness is not a staple of man.
It was, however, in God's first plan.
He created us in grand perfection.
We preferred a different direction.

19

God's Forgiveness

Is there one, Lord, you have not forgiven?
To the edges of the universe there are none!
Grant in me your God forgiveness
That I too may harbor no ill will.
That I may flourish as a flower in your garden.
Write in my mind your statutes.

Teach me your rules,
The rule of LOVE
And a forgiving heart.
Teach me to surrender—to serve
With a servant heart,
With Joy
With Love
And a forgiving heart.
Erase from my mind, my soul, my spirit
Those memories of actions I allow to hurt
To irritate me.
Give me
A Forgiving heart.
I LOVE YOU
You are more that enough.

20

A SLEEPLESS NIGHT

I was experiencing a sleepless night. My tired tank was full; I sensed that all was right. Sleep, however, did not come to meet my expectancy. I quietly prayed, oblivious to the person lying next to me.

I prayed for all of those on my short list of prayer. It included my wife, our children, both Spiritual and biological. Sleep still wasn't there. I prayed on my left side, then, I prayed on my right. I became aware that I might be awake until I got it the way God wanted it tonight. Perhaps my approach was wrong from the beginning. Was I guilty of talking when I should be listening? I opened my eyes and observed my surroundings. I glanced out the window and peered about the room. It was a place lighted by soft shafts of light emanating from a partly cloudy moon. Then God embellished my perception with His perfection and all beauty was enhanced. I saw what I had missed with my first natural glance.

He showed me His daughter. She was within inches of me, sleeping, profoundly embraced by His Peace. She was laying on her side, facing toward me, clasped hands beneath her chin, a perfect reflection of God's Peace within. Her countenance projected the beauty of God's contentment. It was contentment that He seemed to have given gracefully in return for her commitment. There came an increasing awareness inside of me of an eternal Spiritual beauty dwelling in the one so close beside me.

There was no sound or gesture. I knew with certainty that God loved her fervently. My urge was to touch her and to speak. I wanted to communicate that it was not God alone who loved her. I lay there in consternation, not wanting to disturb His interaction with His creation.

Finally, gently, cautiously I reached out and laid my hand on her side. I shared with God my precious bride.

It is my hope to remember this night the rest of my days through eternity. And spend those days praising God for sharing His moment with me.

21

Great Are You

Lord I praise you,
all of my days I praise you,
My soul praises you.
Lord "HELP."
I can do nothing without you.
When I'm alone, I am powerless in a hostile environment.
Great are you,
you are the source of all good,
all power, all character,
you are willing,
you are the Creator,
you are the giver,
Please empower me to receive,
Please teach me your ways for my life,
Please teach me to teach, to love,
and to present others to your empowerment!

22

HE IS THE ONLY ONE

Many men have bled for a cause.
HE is the only one whose blood cleansed us from sin.
Many men have been tortured and beaten.
HE is the only one by whose stripes we are healed.
Many innocent men have had their bodies broken.
HE is the only one whose beaten body became the Bread of Life.

Many men have begged for forgiveness.
HE is the only one who forgave us.
Many men have sought after God.
HE is the only one who gave us access to God.
Many men have been placed in a grave.
HE is the only one who, of His own accord, arose from it.
Many men have died on the cross.
HE is the only one who is God—The Great I AM.

23

THEY SAID HE'S DEAD

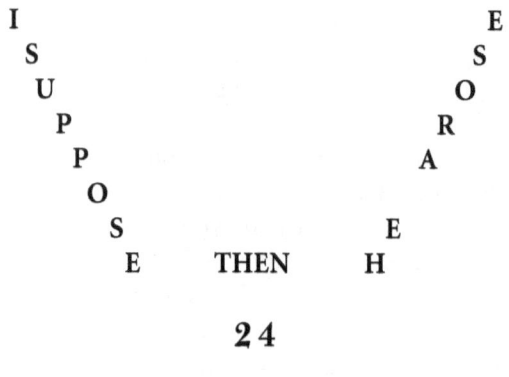

24

Good News

The bad new is, the world has fallen.
Never on its own will it come back again.
It's lower than ever before.
Each day, it sinks a little bit lower.

This continued decline is not a given.
This world could become a lot like heaven.
Perpetual darkness it not a given.
The good news is, the Son has risen.

25

I Will Give You All My Worship

I will worship You with all of my heart.
I will praise You with all of my strength.
I will seek You all of my days.
I will follow all of Your ways.
I will give You all my worship.
I will give You all my praise.
You alone I long to worship.
You alone are worthy of my praise.
I will bow down and hail You as King.
I will serve You, give You everything.
I will lift up my eyes to Your throne.
I will trust You, will trust You alone.

26

My Empowerment

Lord, Help.
I can do nothing without You.
Alone,
I am powerless, in a hostile environment.
Great are You,
You are the source of all good,
all character, and all power.
You are willing,
the Creator, the giver of all good Gifts.

Please, empower me.
Please, teach me
your ways for my life.
You are the Teacher.
Please, teach me to teach, teach me to love.
Teach me to introduce others
to Your Empowerment.

2 7

Only Grace

I wept today as I stood in this place
And considered who I am, weighed against who God is.
I stood and pondered and experienced His Grace.
In spite of my sense of the difference, I found myself in His Presence.
Then I reviewed my shortcomings (those of which I'm aware),
Failures as a father, a farmer, a husband, a friend.
It made no difference to Him, He was still there.
How could He know of this and bless without end?
How could He bless me in such tangible ways,
Three children alive, well prepared as saints?
Those and a wife who has loved me all my days.
He even changed my character traits.
I wept today as I stood in this place
And considered who I am, weighed against who God is.

2 8

The Edge

I walked one day, I walked to the edge,
An emotional precipice, a vertical ledge.

Again and again, I return to where I'd begun,
Each trip more difficult than the previous one.

I walk to the edge, and take in the view,
A view always changing, a view never new.

Standing at the edge I see strife and distress,
Some perceived, all real, nevertheless.

Each trip out seems to increase in cost.
Sometimes an unfortunate tragedy, always a personal loss.

There is a void past the edge, the dangers are real,
No scream will help, no personal appeal.

As I view from this position
I observe a strange and new condition.

What appeared at first to be a vast, empty expanse, is a view of
Eternity, time, and space mixed together, an incomprehensible mass.

The view from the edge is of unfathomable scope
The question becomes, "Where lies my hope?"

The walk to the edge comes all too often,
That time to cry at an open coffin.

Face to face at the edge, face to face with the ultimate cost,
The cost of love, the cost of the cross.

When I walk to the edge, I see a father paying the price,
The price of a Son, as a sacrifice.

The walk to the edge comes all too often
That time to cry at an open coffin.

29

Spiritual Survival

When you have nothing to do
And your mind is all empty,
Find yourself a pen or two and
Write the words all down, be there few or many.
We are not creatures of chance.
Until the fall
We didn't even wear pants
Or fig leaves at all.

We certainly aren't great.
We're not even good.
Even in a welfare state,
Who is the one furnishing the food?
In a world of education
And great intellect,

Life is no vacation,
And the world is a wreck.

Do we grow?
Or do we try?
Tantrums we throw
As we sit and cry.
Though His peace
Is in the valley,
We wallow in dirt and grease
In the devil's back alley.

Why do we fight it?
The price is all paid.
To the angels delight,
We can all make the grade.
By God's choice
Noah survived the flood.
We survive day to day
By His grace and His blood.

3 1

It Couldn't Be

Jere and his lifelong friend, Jack Lane (now deceased)

With all our childhood dreams,
Our fantasies,
Never this!
It couldn't be.
How could one
Be so bold
To even suggest
We were growing old?
It is even more difficult
To explain
If you're the one chosen
To remain.

We weren't ever going
To die.
Not he,
Not I.

32

Special Things in Life

Things are special in life:
Children and health and
An extraordinary wife
Are an enormous wealth.

Here are intimate talks
About children's cares,
And quite walks,
Discussing which responsibilities are theirs.

We look way out
Or search deep within.
We need to ask, "What is the kingdom all about?"
If we want to find Him.

He's there when we search,
If we look for His Kingdom,
Instead of a church,
We will surely find Him.

God puts it together
Way in advance.
To find some other
There if hardly a chance.

Section IV
Fun

1

Now What

It is all so simple upon looking back, if
They would just paint those white lines black.
Then this highway would look like a railroad track.
Though such a decision would meet with derision
At the highway commission, what do they know?
Imagine how those lines would show
The edge of the road in contrast with snow.

2

Jonah the Twenty-Third

Once upon a time there was a bedbug. His name was Jonah the Twenty-third. They all called him that, because he could trace his ancestors clear back for twenty-three generations. He had a bedbug ancestor who traveled across the ocean with a man named Jonah. They crossed it in the belly of a whale. Actually Jonah (the man) was in the belly of the whale, the bedbug was in Jonah's underwear.

Every generation after that was partial to water and did a lot of traveling by ship. They continued the tradition of traveling in people's underwear, of course. When the twentieth century came along and water beds were invented most of the bugs adapted to them and quit traveling so much. This preference for waterbeds is what distinguished the "Jonah" line from all other bedbugs. They do still have a "thing" about traveling in underwear as long as they can sleep in their own waterbed at night.

Well "Old 23," as we lovingly referred to him, set up housekeeping in our waterbed years ago. He minded his own business, and he didn't take up much room. Getting along with him has really been quite easy. Actually his bark was much worse than his bite. He became like a very, very small part of our family, what with our youngest child gone and all.

Last Friday someone left their dumb spiders in our waterbed. That made "Old 23" really mad. He has been gone every since. We don't know if he left forever in someone's underwear, or if he has taken refuge somewhere while he plots his revenge.

If he is planning revenge, I'm sure glad those weren't my spiders!!!!!!!

3

I Missed It

Life has gone on,
even though I resisted.
When the curve in the road came
——————-I missed it.——————

4

What Time Is It?

IS IT A.M.?
IS IT P.M.?
The faces are the same
Since we entered this situation.

I am not sure this has all been fun.
What a boring meeting.
The only one to alter his position
Is the man in the sun.

5

The New Guy in Town

My task for the day was to contact one agency with whom I had no previous contact. My purpose was to establish a working relationship with that agency. This process was to be repeated until all appropriate agency personnel knew who I was and what I did.

Fayette County, Iowa, is unique among the counties to which I am assigned. The county seat is geographically centered but the population center is on the southern edge of the county. The agencies with whom I interact have offices in both places. Some of the agencies have staff in the south on Monday, Wednesday and Friday, others are there on Tuesday and Thursday. Further complications arise in determining if they are there in the morning or afternoon.

My trip began with the possibility of visiting the *Fayette County Relief Office*. (Not working anywhere today.) Another possibility was *Northeast Iowa Community Action* (not in town today either), and the local food pantry.

By default my mission for the day was to contact the *Food Pantry*. With no pun intended I thought this should be a piece of cake.

The food pantry is located in the un-air-conditioned basement of the local Baptist Church. The middle-aged female person in charge eyed me with immediate distrust. I produced one of my Iowa State University Extension Calling cards and introduced myself. She was impressed with neither the calling card nor me. It seems that she closes up for the day at 11:00 A.M. which was very close to the current time. She made it clear that she did not have anything to do with anyone at the Food Bank if the time was not precisely between the hours posted at the entrance. That meant finished at closing time, not starting just before closing time.

I told her that I would like to talk about their referral process as well as their general mode of operation. She brusquely replied that she "don't give referrals." It struck me at this point that things were not going as well as I had hoped. It was interesting to watch her go from a cynical countenance to a "Proud Provider" mode. Having realized that I was a potential referral source she viewed me as a possible helpful ally and supporter of her program. This realization prompted her to promise to mail me forms for my eligible clients. She then graciously toured the facility with me, explained their operating rules and shared her concerns about delivery of services.

It has been my practice to spend part of a day during busy season helping at facilities which I use. We therefore parted amicably with my promise to show up at Thanksgiving. To aid her, of course.

6

Girl Friday

I'm not sure if you realize it, but you have found a rare hybrid spider. They were first developed by the early American Indians. They were developed by crossing the red sheep tick with the black widow spiders. They were known as the red striped widower. All of them were male, so they couldn't reproduce. The largest one ever found weighed in a 17 ¾ A.I.P. (American Indian Pounds).

They were originally developed to use as pillows; however, they had the habit of waking up in the middle of the night and sticking their tentacles up the nostrils and smothering the Indians. Forty-three Indians were found dead before they figured out what was happening. They called the cause of death officially SIDS, Sudden Indian Death Syndrome.

The spiders were then trained to be doorbells on the wigwams. They were put on a ledge above the entrance, and when they saw someone about to enter they would beat themselves on the chest with little drumsticks (from pigeons), so the occupants would know someone was coming. This had to stop after one dead coon, three dead medicine men and one medicine woman were found on the doorstep, who were all beat to death with pigeon drumsticks.

So the Indians got to thinking that they were spiders and sheep ticks crossed and should make really good fiber cobwebs. They also trained them to make tablecloths and doilies. Since they had no tables or chairs to put them on, they quit breeding them and the spiders have been thought extinct since 1391.

7

Boredom

Can boredom be fatal?
Or is it a temporary affliction?
Is this vacuum in my mind meant to last?
Or will it be a short-term condition?

What about this vacant state of mind?
Is it something that can be changed?
Is it a new tradition? Or have I become
Deranged?

8

The Truth about the Birds

Motivational speakers and writers love to tell the story about those birds that fly north every spring, and south again every fall. These birds fly in V-shaped formations. Using assumptions and suppositions, which require incredulous imagination, they tell us how we in groups should do the same things those birds do. I submit the premise that these are convenient myths used by the presenter to make his or her point. I shall attempt to clarify these various myths with my impression of what these birds are really doing. The truth is, they are trying to imitate things they see the human race do. They must have learned something flying over us and observing us twice a year for countless generations.

The "rotation of leadership" myth says that the lead bird position takes more energy, so they rotate at that position to ease the stress on the leader. The fact is that they "rotate leadership" not out of concern for the wellbeing of the leader, but because no one in the group will admit that the bird in front is as qualified to lead as they are. That is also the reason they make so much noise while in flight. They are complaining about the leadership.

The "V" formation myth says that they fly in that way, because the birds ahead break some of the resistance for those following, so that is the most efficient way to go. There are two reasons they use that formation: one is political and the other a matter of personal hygiene. They don't fly directly behind each other because it is the least demanding formation. They fly in a staggered pattern because they don't stop for bathroom breaks. It is a matter of personal cleanliness.

Secondly, the "V" formation, rather than being an aerodynamic phenomenon is a reflection of human politics. When a left and right begin to form, none of those birds will admit that some other bird is more extreme than they are. Therefore, each bird moves a little more to the right or left than the one preceding it.

The last myth I want to deal with says that when one of the birds has to break formation and land, another one goes with it out of some sort of compassion. The fact is, the second bird (known as the enforcer) goes along to tell the first one that there better be something wrong. He has broken tradition by not completing the flight, as all good birds have done since the beginning of time. There is also a fear that it may have found a better way to go through life, and that would force all the other birds to rethink their whole philosophy.

I hope that this helps clarify the misleading motivational stuff.

9

Just East of Osage.

Just east of Osage,
Running right beside the highway,
A power line runs north to south
Designed, I'm sure, to perturb me.
The poles look somewhat familiar
Much as they did in the old days
When they were simply designed in a "T".
Their task, to carry three-phase electricity.
These poles have been modified,
Perhaps the result of an engineer's nightmare.
They resemble nothing ever seen by a lineman
Anytime, anywhere.

A steel extension is bolted to the top.
It has to bow around existing wire
And rise about six more feet
To carry a different line that much higher.

The thing that troubles me
About raising the wire six more feet?
Did they cut the poles too short
Or dig the holes too deep?

1 0

Constant Sorrow

I am proud to inform you that you have been selected to receive a charter membership in the *Constant Sorrow* support group in your community. This is a limited membership in that membership is offered only after the completion of an intensive selection process. When we decide to establish a group in a community, the initial membership is limited to twenty-six. The selection process is quite simple. Each week we open the local telephone directory to a letter. We start at the front of the book and since this is the first week of selection for your community we start with the A's, each week we move to the next letter. We feel this process will assure that we have the kind of diversity that is expected of an honest organization. How coincidental and fortunate for you that your surname starts with an A. The phone book is randomly opened to that correct letter of the alphabet, in this case the A's. Our resident Chimpanzee and vice president in charge of marketing then throws a dart at the open phone book. I am happy to announce to you that today the dart stuck exactly in the circle made by the circle in the top part of the g in your last name. A couple of centimeters higher and you would have been out of luck.

The mission of Constant Sorrow International is to establish a method by which people without appropriate outlets can share. For instance, if your canary succumbs from inhaling fumes from your neighbor's meth lab, we furnish a safe place to lament. The police certainly will not be supportive. Some people have unbelievable workplace happenings that must be shared with a group gullible enough to believe it. These things need to be spread around so that more people will be able to sing the chorus of our amazing theme song.

As the very first charter member of your local group, for just a slight increase in cost, I think I could guarantee you the position of commandant of the group.

You can have the privilege of being the first person in your community to hold such an esteemed position. We are using a sliding scale for enrollment fees. The sliding scale is a concept we borrowed from the local weight-loss club. Weight-loss clubs are one of our biggest suppliers of people in need of a constant sorrow support group.

I hope you seriously consider this rare opportunity. As a matter of fact, this opportunity is so rare that we request that you not forward this offer to anyone. After all who would want to share their sorrow with undeserving people?

We may be one of the few organizations in the world that will acknowledge that their senior staff consists of a Chimp and a Chump.

For more information please feel free to contact the home office, or you can send a letter by US mail and see how that works for you.

11

Here Sit I

"Here sit I, with a song in my heart
And a view of the sky.
This is a brand new day, with an exciting start.

"Thoughts cross my mind in an unusual manner.
The instructions require an action.
The words become more clear.

"Take your view of the sky.
Pass it on as a breath of fresh air.
Pass it on to one who might otherwise cry.

"Take the words of the song,
Pass them on as words of encouragement
To one who might otherwise hear none.

"Here sit I, with a view of the sky
And a song in my heart
Anyone can see the view, or hear the song—if they try."

12

I Don't Know

I sat in the airport lobby
Watching the people come and watching people go.
Some were young, some old
Some moved really fast, some slow.
Some headed east with authority.
Others headed west.
Then they were all gone. In an instant
I was all that I had left.
I sat in the airport lobby
pondering all of this.
It's one more thing for my
"I don't know" list.
It made no difference, fast or slow.
They all left, I watched them go.

13

Ideas

I lay there one night.
Great ideas came
And then they took flight
Leaving me exactly the same as before.
They streamed by like stars
In the galaxy.
With speed exceeding by far
Others which had come to me before.
I saw great and lengthy rhymes,
All in the most superb meter.
Stories for a future time,
Great in stature, worthy of theater.
As happens nearly every night,
I dozed off, they took flight,
As before.

14

Is This Some Day or What?

This a day like any other day.
I can't remember where I am.
I don't remember if I left the clean spoon
In the peanut butter or the jam.
I think I ate popcorn and watched the Super Bowl.
Some team won it,
Either the Titans or the Rams.
My mind is like the filter on a dryer
All clogged up with fuzz.
It has been a day just like any other day.
I don't remember where I was.

15

Kissing the Kleenex

I had a startling revelation
While shaving in the bathroom.
Please don't take it out of context,
But someone's been kissing the Kleenex.

Now I'm the best of sports.
Seldom ever do I get out of sorts.
But I'm sorry that, when I'm not missing,
The Kleenex has been getting all the kissing.

Could it be that I've not been perky?
Or could it be the new beef jerky?
It takes more than breath savers to smother
That excellent jerky from Catleno Bros.

How about the lack of winking?
Anything to do with my pipe stinking?
When I've been missing kisses
It is of necessity to be brief.

Could it have anything to do
With the plaque on my teeth?

16

April in South Dakota

We brave souls ventured to South Dakota
Back in the spring of '95.
We planned an Easter visit,
We barely escaped alive.
Perhaps the visit was ill conceived.
Winter was still prowling around,
Refusing in its stubbornness
To leave those people alone.

The problem became manifest
When we turned north at Sioux Falls.
Mother cows shivered in snow drifts.
Newborn calves wore coveralls.
The first night there was tough,
Though we were not strangers here
We'd come straight from Iowa,
Without our winter gear.

The top cover was light and airy
Like the stuff on a lemon pie, mostly fluff.
Effort to ignite a romantic fire failed.
It had gone out somewhere around Council Bluffs.
A search for covers began
Frosty feet clinked on the tile floor.
Not the only one becoming inanimate
Surely there will be more.

There must be blankets in this basement
To keep us all from the casket.
Exploring in the dark, I fell on a second bed
My head had made contact with a low-hanging basketball basket.

My head became more clear,
Like a space ship on reentry.
I'll take all of these covers
To cover us up so gently.
My body temperature began
Its climb back toward my norm.
Now there's just one obstacle to sleep,
A two hour thunderstorm!!!!

17

Patent Pending

They tell me of a mountain that is legendary.
It can't be crossed on foot or by dromedary.
It looms so tall, its height uncounted.
Its slopes uncharted.

Plans to scale it, totally unfounded.
When the sun comes up, it goes around it.
There is a plaque on the summit.
It's been there from the beginning.

On plaque are two words,
"Patent Pending."

18

Flies in Our Bedroom

There were two dang flies in our bedroom. Now it seems like that would be one for Bev and one me. That was not the case, however. They both decided to spend the night on my face. The one on my forehead I was able to kill. I almost knocked myself out doing it. The second one seemed to want to nest on my lips. I felt very uncomfortable *inhaling* and was afraid to hit myself in the mouth.

I thought it was time to get creative so I laid the edge of the sheet over my lips leaving my nose exposed. This worked real well until Bev rolled over. Apparently she hangs unto the sheet with both bands when she rolls over. The sheet left my side of the bed at an approximate speed of eighty-eight feet per second. Both lips got second degree burns from the friction of the sheet passing across them.

The nose was a different story. The edge of the sheet was a little rough, kind of like a cloth saw blade. I thought just briefly that I was going to have to have a nose transplant. I'll swear I could hear the fly *laughing.*

I departed the bed for the kitchen where I found a spray can of "OFF." I applied it liberally to all exposed skin and returned to bed with "OFF" dripping from me. When I crawled back in bed the fly was no longer laughing, but Bev was. She laid there and giggled. Some folks are easy to entertain.

19

Prince

Jere and Prince

Every boy who
Isn't a phony
In a flash of ignorance
Asks for a pony.

I had asked
Even begged

Maybe even offered
An arm and a leg.

Came the Christmas
Years after, begging forgotten
I found that
A brand new pony I'd gotten.

I'm proud to proclaim
There was sufficient grace
Not to tell them that now I'd prefer
A bike in his place.

We waited his arrival.
Prince, was his name.
An unbroken colt
When he came.

Half Shetland and Arabian
He was pretty to see.
As it turned out,
A lot smarter than me.

It was soon apparent,
No matter what I contemplated,
He had no intention
Of being domesticated.

He was a two-gaited pony
Like it or not
One gait was as fast as he could go
And the other gait was instantly ... stopped.

He could see a tree limb
Which would just clear his back
And run under it unerringly
Like a train on a track.
He could open any door
That was left unattended,

Letting out livestock
The way he intended.

One habit he had
That got my goat.
Upon seeing a mud hole
He thought I should float.

Our long running feud
Lasted for years.
His final demise
Brought me no tears.

When I discovered
Cars and filling stations
We turned him into
Pelleted rations.

His ultimate fate
Was for me to choose.
We transformed him
Into fox feed and glue.

20

Where Lilacs Grow

People make strange choices, as they walk through life,
Have you ever wondered how she ended up with THAT husband?
Or, he with that wife?

Some choose to live in the desert, of the great Southwest,
Where strange looking creatures crawl all around.
And cactus does best.

Some refuse to give consequences a second thought.
They build their homes, and raise the kids,
On the San Andreas Fault.

Mr. Kilmer became famous for a poem, a poem about a tree.
He can think that way, if he wants, that is his choice.
But that's not me.

I don't care if it thunders or rains where I live. I don't care if it snows.
I don't care if the terrain is forbidding, the world, condescending.
I chose to live where lilacs grow.

I can look where great-grandmother looked, a long time ago.
I can stand in the very same place she stood, and watch
Those lilacs grow.

The time is coming when I'll live in a Mansion, streets will be GOLD.
That's a result of Grace, and I am thankful. Today I am thankful for life.
And to live where lilacs grow.

21

What I'd Rather Be

It is obvious from the start "Hound-dog" is taken.
Anyway, Elvis sang about that, if I'm not mistaken.
It took seven years at the start of my time,
For my parents to decide which species was mine.
Now I'm asked by one of the throng,
What would I be if my parents were wrong?
There are horses, cows, and things like that.
I'd rather be anything than a self-centered cat.
There are pigs and sheep and stinky old goats.
There are beaver and mink that they make into coats.
Those are things I don't want to be, I've cleared that hurdle.
I think if I can't be me, I'd be a turtle.
They're not easily injured, their skin in thick.
They don't worry about covering the rear, just pull in their neck.
No one tries to ride them, it is seldom the case.
And even more rarely are they put in a race.
They are not bothered by natural disaster, never seen fighting,
And I've yet to hear of one that was struck by lightning.
They adapt to sea or land without even trying.
From what I've heard it is seldom that you see one flying.

Without a thought of diet, their life span is nifty.
Don't plan for retirement till they are three hundred and fifty.
I think, my friend, I have said enough to support this.
All things considered, I'd be a tortoise.

22

Seldom is Seldom

Seldom is seldom
More seldom than
When frequent seems
Seldom.

Not often is for priests
And preachers,
Not for students
And teachers.

Kids underfoot
And time is flying.
I won't quit, though,
I keep on trying.

23

Charley and Farm Dog

Charley was an Iowa farmer, a Bohemian by heritage.
Charley wasn't concerned about being politically correct.
In his view, "Bohemian" is the best thing you could call him.
Unless, of course, you called him Czech.

Now Charley's dog started life as a house dog.
He sort of ran things just the way he liked.
He was a dog living in a people house,
Then a new house came down the pike.

Mrs. Charley drew the line.
"Get that dog out," she said,

"His name is now Farmdog.
His other choice is to be dead."

Farmdog moved outside
Where he started a new career.
Far as he could see or run was his domain.
Or so it appeared.

He and Charley farmed the farm.
The best of friends became.
They worked the farm on sunny days.
They went to town when it rained.

Old Farmdog supervised
The planting of the crops and the tilling of the soil.
He was there when they raked the hay
And when they changed the oil.

Farmdog came up lame
in the summer of '93.
It might have been his foot.
It could have been his knee.

He carried that leg most of the spring,
Until the weather was "dog days" hot.
Charley decided it was time for a trip to the vet.
Whether Farmdog liked it or not.

There are two stops in the town,
According to Farmdog's canine mind.
The elevator was the first,
Followed by a tavern down the line.

A fat lady in white behind the counter,
Took care of veterinary "reception."
Every door in the place was open
On this hot day, for cross ventilation.

Jere Probert

There is a statement about vet clinics
That is always true.
When the weather gets really hot,
They smell like a pharmacy crossed with a zoo.

Charley parked in front of the Vet's.
Farmdog saw the open door.
He didn't know where they were going.
This was a new place to explore.

They made their entrance.
Charley began to explain ...
"I know he is a farm dog," the fat lad growled,
"Now tell me his name."

Charley flicked cigar ashes on the floor,
And said something expedient.
Old Farmdog saw the open doors, and
He promptly forgot the word obedient.

He hastened on three good legs to mark out all he could see.
A brand new territory.
All the way from the garage to that
Veterinarian's laboratory.

It was his hind leg that was bad.
I must pause to explain.
Convenient, for the task at hand,
Raising it caused no greater pain.

Every examination room,
Every hallway he explored
Every door he marked uniquely,
As well as the place where medicine is stored.

He wrote in dog language,
Without malice or strife,
At every one of his stops
The Bohemian philosophy of life.

"Bring him in, Charley, it's his turn."
While Farmdog made his round and was treated by the vet
Some new events transpired.
The fun hadn't even started yet.

In the middle of the waiting room,
There, just sitting in the breeze,
Was this pretty young lady
With shorts way above the knees.

There, all combed and brushed
Taking a sickly nap,
Like Farmdog's answered dream,
Was a Siamese cat upon her lap.

Getting down low
Farmdog's plan was instantly in mind.
Just sneak in quietly
He would attack from behind.

He looked around
And approached the unsuspecting pair.
His instinct in full command
He slipped beneath the chair.

The implementation was perfect,
Quiet as the hot breeze.
He shoved his slimy muzzle
Up the thigh side of her knees.

The cat came to attention
On the top side of her thighs
Claws fully extended.
The young thing leaped to her feet, with saucer looking eyes.

Her sick cat just stuck there,
As if its paws were super-glued.
The vet came in horrified
Like a man about to be sued.

"Come on Farmdog."
Charley strolled toward the door.
"We've two more stops to make,
And it's almost time to chore.

2 4

My Song

Did I do wrong when I sang my song?
Was it not appreciated?
That thing I created.
Did I sing it too loud?
Did I irritate the crowd?

2 5

Hands Are All Grease

Hands are all grease,
Stains on my teeth,
I'm really a nice guy
… underneath.
Hands Are All Grease

2 6

Sometimes in a Boy's Life

Sometime in a boy's life
Between electric trains
And girls, should be a time
To develop some brains.

2 7

On Romance

There is a time to be romantic.
It should say that in the Bible.

I am sure it could be there as well.
That there is a time to be Contrite.
Like changing the clocks in the spring and fall
Romance requires action with discipline and
It seems to be at least one day too late
When I finally get it right.

2 8

What Do You Do?

What do you do
When you can't hear?
What do you do
If your seat is in the rear?

2 9

More Stray Thoughts

When one is tall, one is short
It always brings quite a chuckle
When she aims at his lips,
And hits his belt buckle.

3 0

Money Is Great

Money is great.
Love is greater.
If she offers you both
Take her.